WITHDRAWN

Vector Graphics a I on

RotoVision

Vector Graphics and Illustration

A Master Class in Digital Image-Making

Jack Harris and Steven Withrow

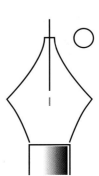

A RotoVision Book

Published and distributed by RotoVision SA
Route Suisse 9
CH-1295 Mies
Switzerland

RotoVision SA
Sales and Editorial Office
Sheridan House, 114 Western Road
Hove BN3 1DD, UK

Tel: +44 (0)1273 72 72 68
Fax: +44 (0)1273 72 72 69
www.rotovision.com

Copyright © RotoVision SA 2008

10 9 8 7 6 5 4 3 2 1

ISBN: 978-2-88893-011-2

Art Director for RotoVision: Tony Seddon
Design: compoundEye

Printed in China by 1010 Printing International Ltd

hooray for diversity

thanks a lot, intelligent design

old school

Contents

Introduction

At the most elementary level, a vector is a series of coordinates and numbers that describe the attributes (such as position, size, and color) of graphics in a 2D space. This technique offers resolution independence and generally smaller files than its bitmap predecessors. Initiated by Adobe's development of its PostScript page description language in the early 1980s, vector-editing software evolved from the earliest bitmap editors, and artists from every discipline and every part of the world soon discovered the flexibility and value of vectors.

The implementation of vector technology in fields as diverse as illustration, type design, animation, and interactive design has allowed artists to leverage their basic knowledge and apply it as they move from one program to another. However, few texts beyond software manuals and an array of specialist magazines have surveyed this important creative area and brought its primary materials and methods to the forefront.

In this book, we explore the many advantages and challenges of vector work and attempt to demystify the unique qualities of vector graphics, by explaining a range of creative processes, and how vector graphics relate to other styles and techniques.

To tell that story, we feature inspiring work from top international illustrators and designers—from the USA and Europe to the Pacific Rim and beyond—along with detailed step-by-step tutorials, artist profiles, and professional advice, useful to the student just starting out, as well as the practicing professional.

We offer more than a "how to" manual; we also examine the "why" of vector art, the thought processes and the choices made by experienced artists at every creative stage.

A map of the book

Section 1, Introducing Vectors, outlines the basic vocabulary of vector art and surveys the great range of vector approaches now practiced around the world, showing how vector techniques contrast and combine with bitmap art.

Sections 2 through 6 form the core of the book, presenting a single continuous tutorial that introduces the ins and outs and nuts and bolts of every step needed to create a professional vector illustration. Using the "ProtoBot project" as a hypothetical example, these five sections explore everything from using the pen tool—the most fundamental step in working with vectors—to integrating bitmap elements and designing a logo. Included within the step-by-step workthroughs are illustrated profiles of talented artists and designers in various fields and

from a range of countries, demonstrating the stylistic and technical breadth of contemporary vector art. Section 7, Other Common Applications, takes a closer look at working with vectors for print and web projects, touches on the popular fields of information graphics and pictorial narratives, offers a glimpse of what is possible in Adobe Flash animation, and includes five additional artist profiles.

Section 8, Additional Resources, provides a valuable reference guide and a glossary of useful terms.

We hope you enjoy this visual journey through the ever-changing and awe-inspiring world of vector graphics and illustration!

1 & 2. Two images from New Zealand–based artist Onno Knuvers (onnoknuvers.com). The first is part of the Metal Man Project (metalmanproject.com), an online collaboration with several other artists. The second, Birds in Tree, was created in Adobe Illustrator for a stationery company.

Images © 2007 Onno Knuvers.

2

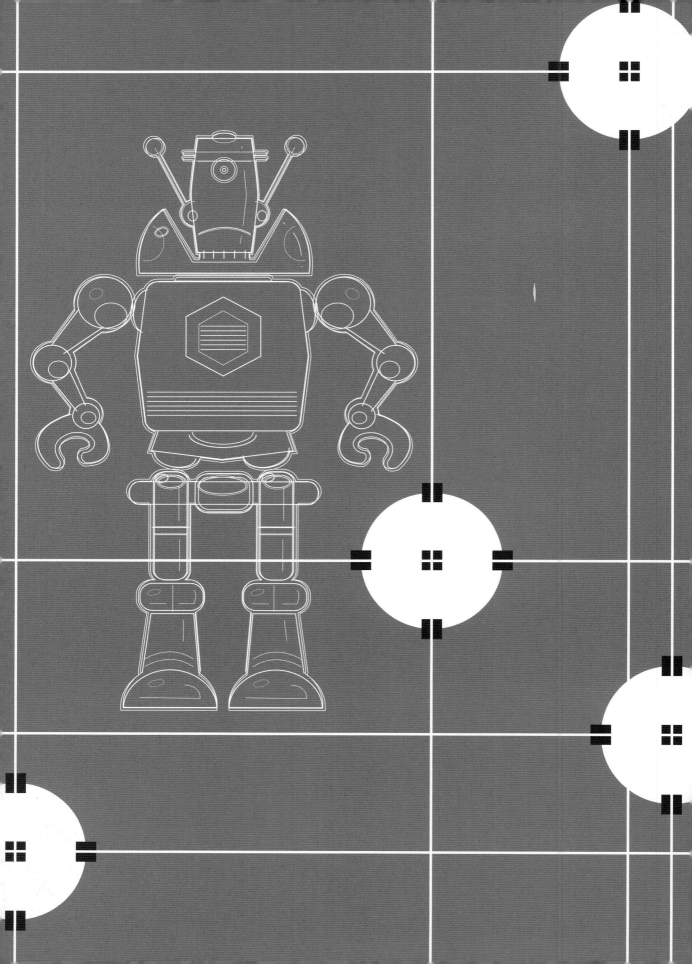

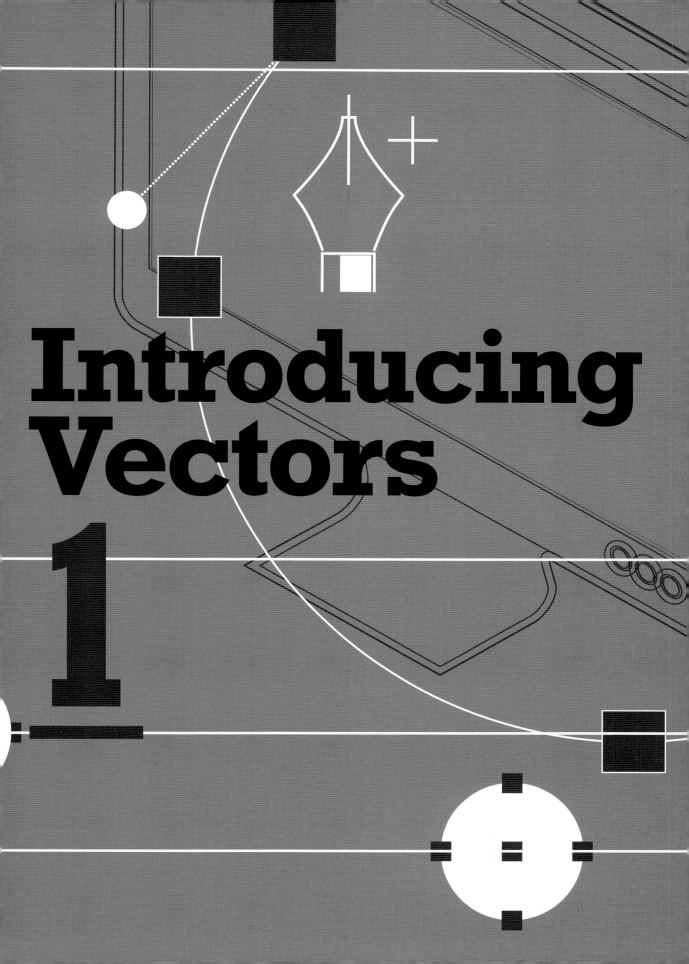

Introducing Vectors

1

The Basics

Vector graphics are a powerful part of contemporary illustration and design. Each day around the world, designers and illustrators use vectors to create unique, high-impact work for nearly every artistic field, including information graphics, website design, logo and character design, technical drawing, comics and graphic novels, children's books, magazine illustration, toy and textile design, and animation.

What are vector graphics?

Vector graphics is the use of "geometrical primitives" such as points, lines, curves, and polygons, which are all based on mathematical equations, to represent digital images. Vector graphics files contain only the information needed to describe an object or shape with the minimum amount of data possible. For a line segment, this information might be as simple as the coordinates of the starting point and endpoint, the thickness of the line, and the color of the line. This creates images that are efficient to render on-screen and in print.

By way of contrast, consider how bitmap images work. They store up to as much as 32 bits of data to describe the color and value of a single pixel. A 10-pixel-by-10-pixel image is made up of 100 pixels, and each pixel has 32 bits of data to describe its characteristics. This means that a 100-pixel-square image contains as much as 1024 bits of data. Raster images can become very large files. In addition, the smaller vector graphic files—memory-efficient, easy to print, and quick to email—can be enlarged or reduced as much as required without the loss of resolution that occurs with pixel-based bitmap or raster images.

Vector-editing programs, such as Adobe Illustrator, CorelDRAW, and FreeHand, complement the capabilities of bitmap editors such as Adobe Photoshop. Vector editors are typically more suitable for graphic design, page layout, typography, and sharp-edged illustrations. Many of these programs also can automatically convert from bitmap to vector graphics and offer the option to combine the vectors and bitmaps in the same file (as do many bitmap-based applications). This combines the best of both worlds in a single file: the precision of a vector (typography, for instance), and the painterly, organic aspects of a bitmap editor.

1. **Coffee Time illustration for MRM Worldwide by Spanish artist Iker Ayestarán (see pages 46 and 47).** *Image © 2007 Iker Ayestarán.*
2. **Yellow Boots poster by British artist Rian Hughes for Jun Co. in Japan (see pages 110 and 111).** *Image © 2007 Rian Hughes.*
3. **Advertising graphics by Swiss designer, cartoonist, and illustrator Demian Vogler.** *[www.demian5.com] Image © 2007 Demian Vogler.*

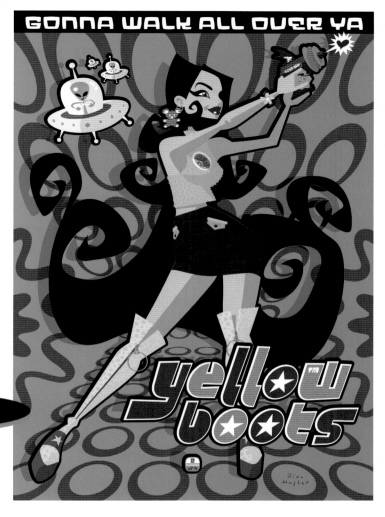

2

Vectors in other applications

More specialized programs such as Flash and After Effects (both from Adobe) are ideal for producing 2D animated graphics. They offer slightly different vector technology to achieve movement and animation. Adobe Flash in particular includes many of the features and functions expected from other vector applications, but also offers an assortment of primitives and drawing tools that include additional behaviors not found in Adobe Illustrator.

Font design has evolved from a typically tedious and expensive process practiced by few to an area of significant growth in design that is practiced by many. Specialized vector programs, such as Fontographer and FontLab, offer another implementation of vector drawing specific to the creation of letterforms. They offer talented and ambitious artists and designers a low-cost opportunity to engage in this specialized aspect of design. In addition, virtually all modern 3D modeling applications offer the ability for artists to create imagery using tools that have a conceptual relationship to vector graphics. Many of the tools work in a similar fashion, and the data necessary to represent a 3D object in virtual space use a similar coordinate-based system.

Although not all vector editors are identical, they feature the same basic tools and approaches to creating images, and they all offer the same critical advantages: resolution independence, small file size, and extraordinary flexibility for change and creative exploration.

3

Vectors and Bitmaps

A simple way to describe the key difference between vectors and bitmaps is to say that bitmaps are composed of a grid of pixels (picture elements; tiny dots of individual shade or color) that combine to form an image, whereas vectors are composed of mathematically defined paths (see Section 2).

Bitmaps, which are resolution-dependent and lose image quality when they are made larger in size, include all images that are scanned, as well as those imported from a digital camera. By comparison, vectors must be created in software, unless they are converted from bitmap images that have been traced or "vectorized." A vector can be easily converted to a bitmap, but in doing so you immediately sacrifice the vector's scalability and resolution independence.

Scaling a bitmap to a larger size ordinarily causes a jagged appearance when viewed on-screen at 72ppi (pixels per inch), but this can be minimized by saving the image at a higher resolution and by using "anti-aliasing"—whereby a program such as Adobe Photoshop gives the appearance of a smooth

border by adjusting the subtle transitions in shading between pixels at the edges of text or a graphic. Vector images need no anti-aliasing and always render at the highest quality.

Unlike vector images, bitmap images are restricted to a rectangular shape and do not support transparency (except in .gif and .png formats for the web). Vector objects can be placed over other objects, and the underlying object will show through.

Common bitmap file formats include .jpg and .gif for the web and .tif and .eps for print. Vector file formats include .ai (Adobe Illustrator), .cdr (CorelDRAW), .dxf (AutoCAD), .wmf (Windows Metafile), and .swf (Adobe Flash). When using a vector file in a program that does not support native vector files, you can save the image as an .eps (Encapsulated PostScript) file, which is supported by most graphics applications. Another option, especially when emailing files or distributing them over the web, is to save the image as a .pdf (Adobe Portable Document Format) file.

When are vectors particularly beneficial?

* When creating detailed, precise, clean illustrations, logos, and icons for print or digital (web/TV/movie/kiosk) design output.
* When creating an animation in Adobe Flash or Adobe After Effects. (Bitmap images can only be imported into these applications and will degrade in resolution with any manipulation.)
* When creating a logo, icon, or illustration that will be needed in multiple sizes, from as small as a thumbnail (useful for the tiny screens of mobile devices) to as large as a billboard.
* When creating graphics that will be shown on high-resolution screens such as high-end monitors or HDTVs.
* When creating characters that will comprise a new typeface/font.
* When manipulating type, creating logos or logotypes, or any other precise, tight-lined graphic or iconography.

3

4

1. **Les Petits Gâteaux: Postcard by San Francisco–based artist Isabelle Dervaux (isabelledervaux.com) for La Boulange, a San Francisco bakery.** © 2007 Isabelle Dervaux.
2. **Illustration by New York City–based artist Daniel Pelavin (pelavin.com) for "Strawberry Raspberry Doin' the Bump" margarita mix.** © 2007 Daniel Pelavin.
3. **Cover illustration by Daniel Pelavin for a *Billboard Magazine* issue on the South By Southwest Festival in Austin, Texas.** © 2007 Daniel Pelavin.
4. **Series of spot illustrations by Isabelle Dervaux for the French free magazine *Pili Pili*.** © 2007 Isabelle Dervaux.

When should vectors be avoided?

* For photo touch-up and photorealistic imagery. A vector's solid areas of color or gradients cannot match the complex tones of a photograph.
* In QuarkXPress layout files. Although much of the world is moving to Adobe InDesign for layout, there are still many users of Quark. One reason users are moving away from this software is that Quark does not accept any form of vector-based images for import, whereas InDesign does.
* In Adobe Photoshop. Although Photoshop has vector-based tools built in, this software is not well suited for this functionality, and using these tools can tax your computer's memory. Many artists create vector graphics in Adobe Illustrator (or a similar program) and then import them into Photoshop.

Two notes

* The color will be slightly off once the object is in Photoshop, so you may need to adjust your colors to have it appear in the Photoshop palette; and
* Photoshop CS3 allows you to import a vector image from Illustrator as a "Smart Object," meaning that your vector image is not converted into a fully pixel-based image, and you can resize the object in Photoshop without any loss of image quality, just as you would in Illustrator.

Vector-friendly software

* Adobe® Illustrator®
* CorelDRAW®
* Adobe® Flash®
* Adobe® After Effects®
* FreeHand
* Adobe® Photoshop® (albeit in a limited capacity)
* FontLab's Fontographer
* Autodesk® AutoCAD®
* Deneba Canvas
* Many 3D graphics programs

5. Illustration by Daniel Pelavin for the 1999 movie *Drop Dead Gorgeous* featuring Kirstie Alley, Denise Richards, Kirsten Dunst, and Ellen Barkin. *© 2007 Daniel Pelavin.*

6. Children's T-shirt design by Isabelle Dervaux for the Bay Bread Boulangerie in San Francisco. *© 2007 Isabelle Dervaux.*

7. Direct-mail piece/poster by Isabelle Dervaux for Give Something Back, an office supply company in the Bay Area. *© 2007 Isabelle Dervaux.*

8. Gender-bending Chemicals: Spot illustration by Isabelle Dervaux for *In Balance* newsletter for the nonprofit organization New American Dream. *© 2007 Isabelle Dervaux.*

Converting and Combining

Converting vector images to bitmaps (rasterizing) is much more easily done than the reverse (vectorizing). Opening a vector file in Adobe Photoshop, for example, allows you to specify the size, color, and resolution of the image. However, rasterizing significantly increases the size of the graphic and sacrifices the scalability and other unique vector qualities of the initial image.

1

Conversely, opening a bitmap image in Adobe Illustrator requires you to "trace" the image to convert it to a vector. Tracing "by hand" means importing a bitmap image into a vector program and using the pen, shape, and line tools to recreate the bitmap piece by piece.

For complex images, many artists utilize the auto-tracing tools available in most current vector applications. Adobe Illustrator's Live Trace, for example, has settings to accommodate photos, grayscale images, hand-drawn sketches, highly detailed illustrations, comics art, technical drawings, black-and-white logos, inked drawings, and typography. Within each of these default groupings, you can adjust the level of detail and fine-tune other elements.

Designer Patrick Coyle offers this caveat: "No piece of software is capable of perfect vectorization, and that is less about the quality of programming in the software and more about how no computer can read our minds to know exactly how we need our images created, and for what purpose."

Hybrid images

Although there are many "vector purists" around the world, it is important to realize that vectors and bitmaps do not have to be kept separate. In fact, the interplay of vector and bitmap techniques has led to many wonderful creative experiments, inspiring a popular hybrid form called "vexel art." (Technically, the term "vexel" refers to raster art that imitates vector techniques, but in common usage, vexel art has come to encompass any combination of vector and bitmap.) A file that contains both raster and vector data (e.g., a vector object with a fill attribute consisting of bitmap data) is called a "metafile."

2

16

1. **Artistic Freedom:** Editorial illustration for *ImagineFX*.
2. **Mean Streets:** Editorial illustration for *The Chicago Reader*.
3. **Hercules:** Tutorial image for *Computer Arts*.
4. Portrait of musician Thom Yorke for *The Boston Phoenix*.

All images © 2007 Dave Curd.

3

Dave Curd

Born in Chicago and currently living in Edmond, Oklahoma, Dave Curd (davecurd.com) mentored with illustrator Cameron Eagle at the University of Central Oklahoma before launching his own illustration career. "My technical ability and design sense are self-taught," he says, "but my overall approach to conceptual problem-solving comes from Mr. Eagle."

"I would describe my work as a hybrid between graphic, thick-to-thin strokes and crazy, painterly rendering. It has a forced and hopefully humorous macho element," says Curd. "When I first started working, I wanted to be [comics artist] Charles Burns, but then it dawned on me that art directors would always choose the original over the knockoff, so I never looked back."

Curd's editorial and advertising illustration has attracted a range of clients including *The New Republic*, *The Boston Phoenix*, *Esquire*, *Forbes*, *ImagineFX*, and *Disney Adventures*. He generally works from vector sketch to vector line art to raster rendering, using Adobe Illustrator and Photoshop in tandem. "First and foremost," he says, "I consider myself a vector artist; it's the anchor in everything I do. I just happen to favor coloring in Photoshop. Using them together, I achieve the best of both worlds."

4

Converting and Combining

Artist profile:
Nate Piekos

Country of origin: USA

Primary software: Adobe® Illustrator®, Adobe® Photoshop®, FontLab Studio

Primary fields: Comics, type and logo design, print, web

URLs: blambot.com, piekosarts.com, realmofatland.com

Nate Piekos graduated with a Bachelor's degree in design from Rhode Island College in 1998. Since founding Blambot.com a year later, he has lettered comic books for Marvel Comics, DC Comics, Oni Press, and Dark Horse Comics as well as dozens of independent publishers.

In 2001, he became type designer to award-winning cartoonist Mike "Madman" Allred and has had his designs licensed by such companies as Microsoft, Six Flags Amusement Parks, *The New Yorker*, The Gap, and many others. Piekos's work has also been seen on television and in feature films.

In 2007, he began writing comics professionally with a story in *Hellboy Animated* #3, with more writing projects from Dark Horse and Marvel Comics in the works. His tongue-in-cheek fantasy webcomics series, *ATLAND*, appears at realmofatland.com. When not designing, he is a voracious reader and a dedicated musician. He lives with his wife in New England.

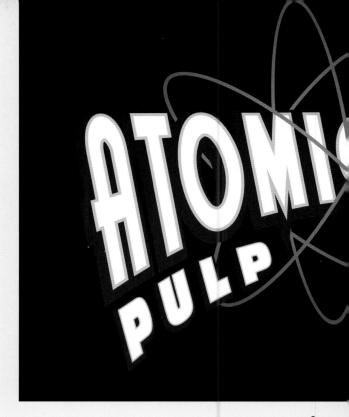

1

2

3

18

Piekos lists letterers Stan Sakai and Todd Klein as his main influences. "I'm not sure if I've developed a recognizable style," he says. "I'd almost hope that I haven't, since being able to create a logo or font in period-specific or genre-specific style is so important. The guiding principle that I reference most frequently for logo design is, 'Make sure it's legible.' An overly designed logo that looks pretty, but can't be read is useless. For fonts, almost anything goes. When I'm happy with it, I know I'm done."

"The perfect typography-based design should be legible and yet enticing to the eye," he continues. "It should serve its purpose as a design element and yet attract someone to want to pick it up and examine it. Imagine walking through the mall and catching a glimpse of some really cool package design.... you might make a point to take a better look at that package. But if you pick it up and you can't READ what's inside, then chances are, you're not going to buy it."

4

PRO SURF SHOP
AD O NI
™
& SKATEBOARDS

5

6

1. Logo design by Piekos for AtomicPulp.com, the online home of writer, editor, and designer Christopher Mills. © and ™ 2007 Christopher Mills.
2. Robot Head logo design. © 2007 Nate Piekos.
3. Heart logo design. © 2007 Nate Piekos.
4. Samurai vector illustration. © 2007 Nate Piekos.
5. T-shirt design. © 2007 Nate Piekos.
6. Logo design by Piekos for DarkCandles.com. © and ™ 2007 Helena Jones.

Artist profile:
Von Glitschka

Country of origin: USA

Primary software: Adobe® Illustrator®, Adobe® Photoshop®

Primary fields: Wide variety of media

URLs: glitschka.com, texturebook.com, illustrationclass.com

"Illustrative designer" Von Glitschka has worked in the communication arts industry for more than 20 years. In 2002, he started Glitschka Studios, a multidisciplinary creative firm based in Salem, Oregon.

Glitschka says that his work reflects "the symbiotic relationship between design and illustration" and that his modus operandi is that of a hired gun for both in-house art departments and medium to large creative agencies, working on projects for such clients as Microsoft, Adobe, Pepsi, Rock & Roll Hall of Fame, Major League Baseball, Hasbro, Bandai Toys, Merck, Allstate Insurance, Disney, Lifetime Television, and HGTV.

1

Ferengi Rule of Acquisition No. 40
She can touch your lobes but never your Latinum.

2

3

20

Glitschka's exuberant graphics have garnered numerous design and illustration awards and have appeared in such publications as *Communication Arts*, *Society of Illustrators*, *Graphis*, *American Illustration*, and *LogoLounge 2*, *3*, and *4*.

Glitschka has authored a book on textures titled *Crumble.Crackle.Burn* (How Books, 2007), and is currently working on his second design book. Glitschka also teaches advanced digital illustration at Chemeketa College and operates the website IllustrationClass.com, where visitors can download free tutorials documenting his illustrative design creative process on a variety of diverse project types. He currently sits on the National Illustration Conference board (ICON5).

Among his artistic influences he lists Jim Flora, *MAD Magazine*, Norman Rockwell, Japanese cartoons, and 1970s pop culture.

4

5

6

1. **Evergreen:** Poster design illustrated for an art show in Mexico.
2. **Ferengi:** *Star Trek* fan art.
3. **Owl:** Illustration created for *Crumble.Crackle.Burn*.
4. **Tiger:** Illustration for a diabetes fundraiser poster.
5. **Vonster:** Self-promotional image created for launch of Vonster.com.
6. **Linear Face:** Illustration created for ad campaign.

All images © 2007 Von Glitschka.

B

C

D

Nuts and Bolts

2

The Protobot Blueprint

By now, the basic concepts and uses of vectors have been adequately covered. Because the programs mentioned vary to a large degree, the tutorials in this book will focus on the most common uses of vector programs: drawing and illustration. Many of the techniques described here will be directly applicable to other vector-based applications.

The format of the tutorial will be loosely based on the fulfillment of a real-world assignment that will allow for demonstration of key concepts and techniques in a specific context. This approach builds on previous steps and allows for gradation from the simple to the more complex. Adobe Illustrator is the model for many of the commands and tools because it has been widely adopted as a standard for this type of work. However, the features demonstrated are common to most vector programs.

Thumbnails.
Critical to the start of any project is the exploration of various solutions. While obvious to many, this step is critical for the beginner. With a good thumbnail, the execution of the art can be the concentration of the process.

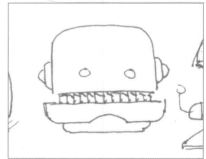

After a thorough exploration, a thumbnail can be chosen and used as the basis for a final pencil drawing of the art.

24

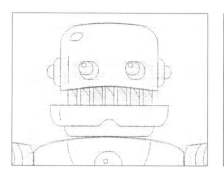

The pencil drawing.
Although it is not necessary to draw every detail in the final pencil drawing, the better developed it is, the easier it is to explore options in the digital drawing process.

Scanning the pencil drawing.
The first step in the process of electronic work is the scan of the pencil drawing. This becomes the blueprint for the development of the illustration.

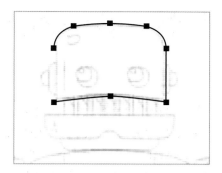

The drawing process.
The art is opened as a template and the pen tool is introduced as the primary drawing tool. Often one of the most difficult tools to learn, the pen is also the most important.

Basic color options and uses.
The options available for color and editing are extensive. Color models are covered with a focus on those color systems used for print reproduction.

Advance color development.
After learning the baseline color features, more complex processes are covered including gradients, shape blends, and gradient meshes.

Special effects.
Vector and bitmap special effects will be explored.

Incorporating bitmap files created by other applications.
Placing bitmap images into the illustration is a common practice and requires special consideration.

Typography.
Vector programs are particularly well-suited to setting and manipulating type. The project will include developing a logo, one of the more common uses of type in a vector format.

Final art.
The conclusion of the development phase will include save and export options as well as various file formats and their uses.

The DNA of Vectors

The smallest building blocks—the point, segment, and path—must be mastered before anything else can be successfully accomplished. The pen tool, which is absolutely critical for success in this environment, is often seen as one of the least intuitive digital drawing tools. Mastery of the pen will ensure a solid foundation for success with other tools as well as an easier transition to other vector-based programs.

These programs tend to be feedback and interface "heavy." The cursors change quickly by context, action, and location. Although some of this visual feedback can be turned on and off in the application preferences, the defaults have been left active and, while not every cursor and interface object is shown, those necessary to understanding a concept are depicted. Recognizing this visual feedback is important in the beginning because of the various uses of each tool.

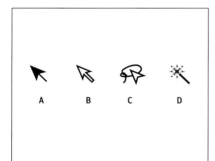

The pointer and selection tools.
A. The pointer and selection tool
B. The direct-select tool
C. The lasso
D. The magic wand
All cursors representing different methods of selecting objects.

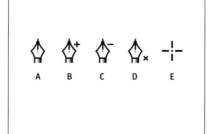

The basic drawing tool: The Pen.
A. The pen tool
B. Add anchor point tool
C. Delete anchor point
D. Context sensitive, this cursor is visible when the first point of a path is created
E. The pointer visible when drawing a primitive

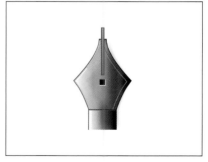

The hammer of vector art.
The pen is the most essential tool in your toolbox.

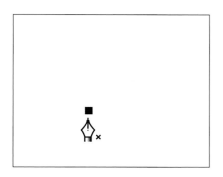

Components of paths.
Clicking once with the pen tool creates a point.
A single point, in and of itself, is not generally
useful. A point is the smallest component
of a segment.

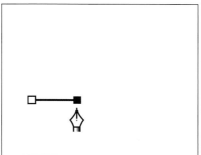

Moving the pen tool to another location and
immediately clicking again creates an endpoint.
The black square indicates an active point. This
is a path and two endpoints.

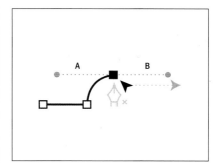

Clicking again, holding and dragging the pen
(the cursor changes to an arrowhead) will create
a smooth point and a segment between the corner
point and the smooth point. A smooth point always
has two direction lines (A, B).

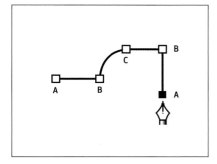

With two more points added, the path now includes
two endpoints (A), two anchor points (B), and a
smooth point (C). The most recent point added is
selected (indicated by the black square).

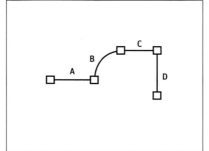

A segment is the smallest component of a path.
This path has four segments (A, B, C, D).

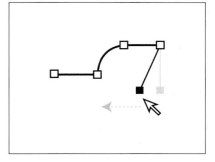

The open pointer is the direct-select tool, used
to select parts of a path like points and segments.
Here the black square indicates a selected point.
The direct selection allows for change to the
selected component without necessarily affecting
the rest of the path.

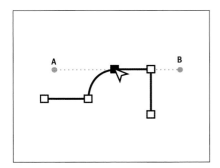

Clicking on the smooth point selects it and makes
the direction lines and their associated direction
points (A, B) visible.

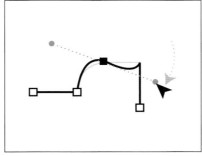

Clicking and dragging on the direction points
modifies the curve's angle, length, and shape.

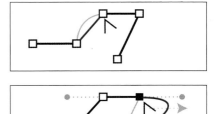

The convert anchor point tool changes a smooth point
into an anchor point with a single click (top). Clicking
and dragging a point with the tool creates a smooth
point (bottom). Because the endpoints of this path
do not connect, it is referred to as an open path.*

* Red in diagrams is for clarity only. It does not indicate the color of the object.

Springs, Pulleys, and Gears

Primitives are readymade objects that can be used to instantly create commonly used shapes. A perfect circle, an octagon, or a five-pointed star are only a click away. Valuable aids for drawing complex mathematical geometry and a suite of modular components useful for creating more complex shapes, primitives are a staple among vector-based creation tools.

Fundamental shapes, such as the ellipse, rectangle, and polygon, as well as specialized, difficult-to-draw objects such as the spiral and star, are included in most vector programs. Programs for animation or 3D applications provide an even greater array of easy-to-use base objects. Without question, these tools provide essential workflow and creative options.

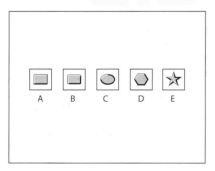

The shape primitives.
A. The rectangle tool
B. The rounded rectangle tool
C. The ellipse tool
D. The polygon tool
E. The star tool

The path tools.
A. The line tool
B. The arc tool
C. The spiral tool

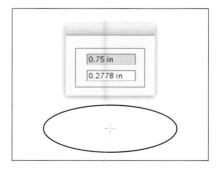

Use numerical control.
All shapes and lines can be created numerically for absolute precision. Click to position the origin point and invoke a dialog box. Input the dimensions of the shape into the height and weight fields and click OK.

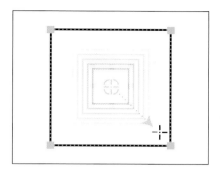

Draw from center.
Choose a tool, press the option key, click to create an origin point and drag in any direction. Pressing the shift key along with the option key constrains the object to increments of 90 degrees. The constraints apply to all shape primitives and lines.

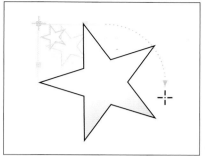

Draw from corner.
Click to create an origin point and drag in any direction to draw your shape. As you draw in an arc, the shape will rotate.

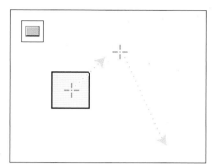

The rectangle tool.
Select the rectangle tool and click in the artwork to set the origin point of the shape and drag.

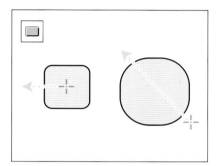

The rounded rectangle.
To adjust the radius of the rounded corners while dragging, use the up arrow to increase the corner radius or the down arrow to decrease it. Shapes can be created by dragging from any corner.

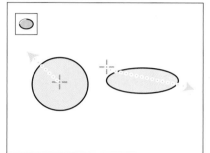

The ellipse.
Select the ellipse tool, click in the artwork to set the origin point of the shape and drag.

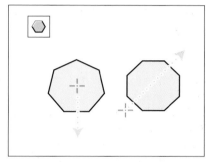

The polygon.
Select the polygon tool, click, and drag. To increase the number of sides while dragging, use the up arrow. The down arrow decreases the number of sides.

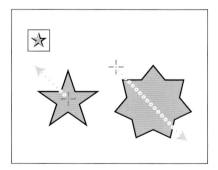

The star.
Select the star tool, click, and drag. In addition to dragging, press the arrow to increase the number of sides. To decrease them, press the down arrow. To increase the sides, press the up arrow; to decrease them, press the down arrow key. Hold down the control (Mac) or Alt (PC) keys to maintain the center radius.

The spiral.
Drag the tool in an arc to rotate the spiral. Hold the up and down arrows to increase or decrease the number of winds in the spiral.

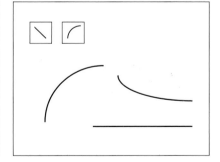

The arc and line.
To draw a line segment, click once to start the line and click again to end the line. The shift key constrains the line to increments of 45 degrees.

The Circuit Board

Points, Segments, and Paths have been demonstrated as the DNA that ultimately allow for the creation of the shapes and objects that are the core of the illustration process. As these various elements are linked, the real power of drawing with vectors can be discovered.

It is with relatively uncomplicated shapes and objects that the primary appeal of vectors is first revealed. Dramatic results can be achieved through the connections made between these simple components. Drawing shapes that are intentional, and that behave predictably, provides the basis for arranging, moving, and manipulating objects in a meaningful way.

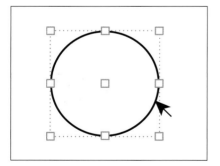

The selection tool or pointer.
After drawing a circle, select it. This reveals its bounding box. The bounding box indicates that an entire object is selected. Clicking and dragging anywhere on the circle—not the bounding box—will move the shape.

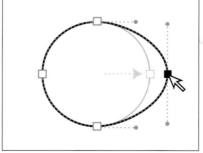

Direct selection of a point on a closed path.
Direct selection of a smooth point allows for direct manipulation of only that point. The point can be repositioned at will. It affects the shape of the path, but does not move the object.

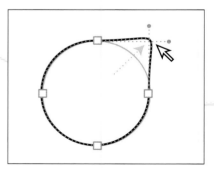

Direct selection of a segment on a closed path.
Direct selection of a segment isolates the segment, allowing manipulation of the segment (and, in this case, the curve), again, without moving the object.

30

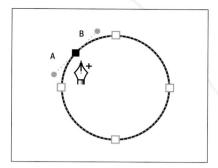

Adding an anchor point to a closed path.
Click on the path with the add anchor point tool. This will create two segments (A and B) out of the original single segment. The path remains closed.

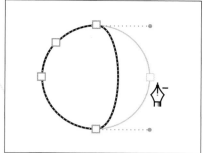

Deleting a point on a path.
Using the delete anchor point tool, click on a single anchor point anywhere on the path. The result can dramatically change the shape, but the path remains closed.

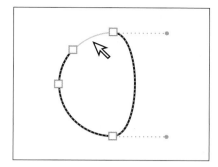

Deleting a segment to create an open path.
Direct-select and cut or delete a segment. This will create an open path. An open path has endpoints.

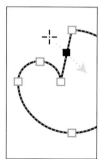 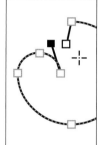

Split a path with the scissor tool.
The scissor tool appears to work similarly to the add anchor point tool (left). In reality it has split the path and created two endpoints (right) that open the path.

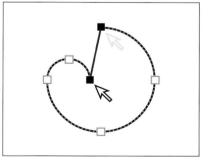

Adding segments to an open path.
Click on an anchor point (A), click and drag to create a smooth point (B), and click a final time to create another endpoint (C).

Filling an open path.
Filling (the shape's color) a shape created by an open path can be deceiving and lead to potential problems. The path looks closed (left), but stroking the path (the line around the shape) reveals the unstroked or open side of the shape.

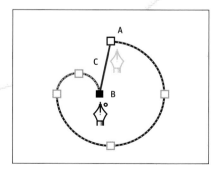

Closing open paths.
An open shape can be closed simply by choosing the pen tool (the little "o" next to the pen indicates the tool is positioned properly over the point) and clicking on one endpoint (A) and then the other (B). The resulting segment (C) joins the two endpoints, completing the path.

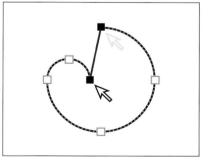

Another common way to close an open shape is, while holding the shift key down, to click once on each endpoint with the direct-select tool. From the Object menu choose Path > Join.

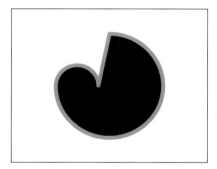

A properly closed shape, filled and stroked, would look like this.

Natural Selection

The concept of selecting objects sounds simple. Although the tools themselves are fairly straightforward, the simple act of choosing a single path or object can be a challenge as an illustration develops.

Precise selection tools enhance productivity and save time. In addition, unique uses of the selection tools can contribute to interesting results. The ability to select and transform discrete pieces of objects (individual points or segments) provides almost limitless editability and tremendous creative opportunities.

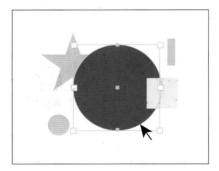

A selection.
A selection is the currently active object(s) and is surrounded by its bounding box. All transformations affect the current selection. To make a selection, click on a shape. To add to a selection, hold down the shift key and click on several shapes. Shift click on a selection to deselect it.

A direct selection.
The direct-selection tool (the open arrow) selects components of objects: points, segments, and paths. The selected anchor point is indicated by the blue square.

Direct-selection tool and shift key.
Multiple direct selections can be made by holding down the shift key and direct-selecting another component. The three blue squares indicate the selection of three points on the star. Shift-clicking will deselect a component.

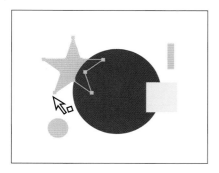

Direct selection of a whole shape.
The direct-selection tool can also be used to select an entire shape by pressing the option key and clicking on the shape. This allows mixed selections of components and shapes.

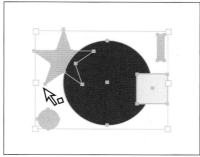

Select All menu choice.
From the select menu, choose select all. This will choose all visible, unlocked objects. Choose deselect from the menu to deselect all.

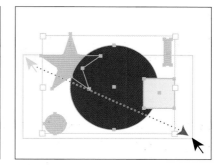

Select all by dragging.
A simple selection can be made by dragging the selection tool around a group of objects. Any object at least partially in the drag area will be selected.

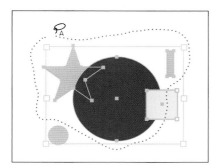

Select by lasso.
Drag the lasso tool around a group of objects to create a selection. Unlike the selection tool, an object that is not completely surrounded by the drag area will only be partially selected. The green square is not completely selected.

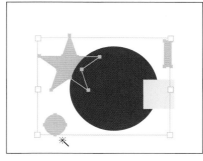

Select with magic wand.
The magic wand selects all visible and unlocked objects that have the same fill color.

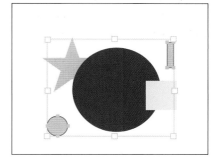

Select by attributes
In the shape menu there is a submenu labeled "same." There are choices to select by identical attributes such as same fill color, same opacity, or same stroke width. Here, the two objects with the same stroke color—red—have been selected.

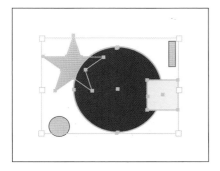

Select inverse.
This menu command deselects everything currently selected and selects any that was not in the previous selection. This diagram is the inverse selection of the previous diagram.

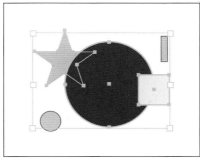

Save selection.
This menu command saves a record of the current selection. The selection can be named and appears in the select menu. This selection has been saved.

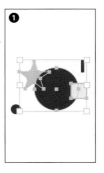

Load saved selection menu item.
After making a different selection (1), the saved selection from the previous figure, is loaded (chosen from the menu) and it is instantly restored as the current selection (2). Saving selections in the design process is a significant productivity boost.

Tutorial:
Enhanced Optics

Control over what appears in the work area is essential. As complexity builds, so too does the need for control of the visibility of individual components.

With finite control over every aspect of the application, the user can hide elements such as the bounding box, guides, grids, and rulers to eliminate visual clutter and clarify the difference between art and interface. Zoom in for microscopic detail and zoom out for the ultimate bird's-eye view. These options provide an impressive array of visibility controls that adjust the delicate balance between the need for interface hints and feedback and the desire for visual clarity as you explore design possibilities.

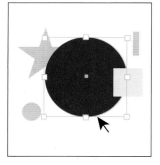 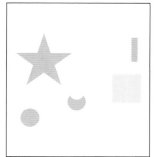  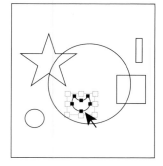

Hide and show.
The hide and show commands in the Object menu are used to hide selected objects or to show all. On the right, the circle has been hidden to reveal another object. Use Hide aids in situations similar to this, where objects may have been "lost," or to easily modify partially covered objects.

Preview and outline modes.
The active window can be set to Preview mode where the art is seen as it will reproduce (left) or set to Outline mode (right). Outline mode displays all objects as black outlines. In Preview mode, colored regions are selectable. In outline view, only the lines are selectable. This is particularly useful when making difficult selections. Preview and Outline are available in the View menu.

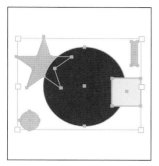 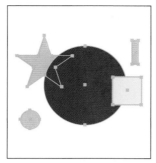 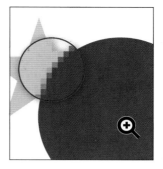 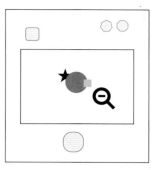

Hide bounding box.

Selected objects display a bounding box by default. On the right, hide bounding box has been chosen from the View menu. The blue squares indicate that the objects are still selected. Hiding the bounding box simplifies the display of objects for easier selection and editing.

Zoom in and zoom out.

The magnifying glass allows users to incrementally zoom in for extreme detail or zoom out to view the entire artboard. Unused objects are commonly pulled off of the artboard during production. Zooming out can help locate errant objects. On the left is a zoomed-in view of a bitmap, with an overlaying vector art of the same image. This clearly demonstrates the difference between the screen display of a bitmap and that of a vector.

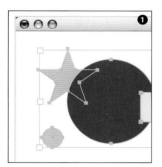 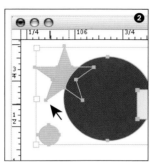 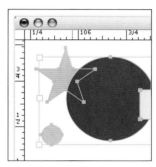 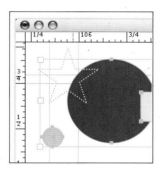

Hide and show rulers.

Rulers are shown and hidden through the commands in the View menu. The rulers also provide the current vertical and horizontal positions of the current cursor. This is represented by the red lines in 2.

Hide and show guides.

Guides can be accessed by clicking and dragging from the rulers. Guides are nonprinting positioning and alignment tools. In addition, almost any object can be converted into a guide (see star at right). Vector art demands extreme precision and the various guide options provide it. Guide visibility and the other guide commands, are found in View > Guides > Submenu.

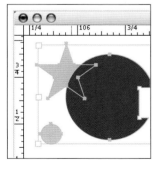 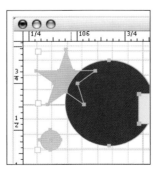 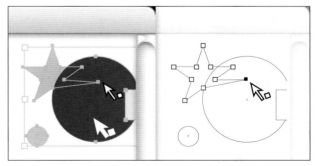

Hide and show grid.

Off by default, grids can be hidden and shown from the View menu. Grid characteristics for a document can be set in preferences.

Two views for simultaneous preview and outline.

By choosing New Window in the Window menu, a duplicate window is created that can have its own view settings. Creating a new window, setting it to Outline mode, and making both windows visible is a powerful editing workspace. Either window can be active. All changes and edits are visible in both windows simultaneously.

Tutorial:
Transformers

With elements completely defined by sets of coordinates and other numerical designations, vectors can be manipulated in ways uniquely their own.

The tools for these transformations are varied, with multiple methods of implementation. They are often used in series to achieve a specific look for an object. A virtually unlimited range of transformations is possible. The basics are presented here with the caveat that, after learning the basic uses of each tool, it is necessary to explore mixing and matching them to fully appreciate the creative opportunities they represent.

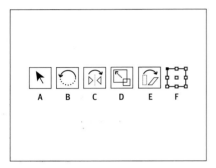

Transform tools.
A. The pointer or selection tool. Move, scale, rotate.
B. Rotation tool.
C. Reflection tool.
D. Scale or resize tool.
E. Shear or skew tool.
F. Origin point indicator.

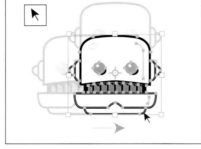

Move by dragging.
Click, hold, and drag an object with the pointer tool. Do not pull on the bounding box controls. Constrain movement to increments of 45 degrees with the Shift key.

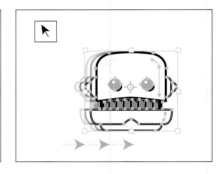

Nudge.
The arrow keys provide for moving a selection in very small increments. Nudge up, down, left, and right based on an increment that can be set in Preferences.

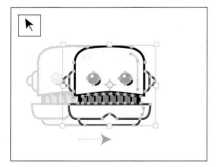

Move with numerical control.
Double-click the pointer in the toolbox. In the resulting dialog, enter in the distance for the desired move and click OK.

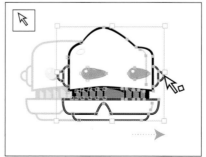

Move direct selection.
Make a selection with the direct-select tool. Clicking and dragging specific points and segments offers another approach to manipulation and transformation.

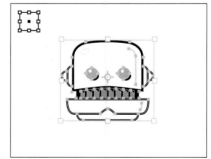

Origin or reference point.
By default, an object's point of origin is its center. To change, make a selection and click once to position the origin point. While there are practical limits, the origin point can be almost anywhere.

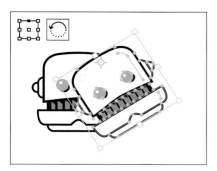

Rotate with numerical control.
Click once with the rotate tool to set an origin point (top middle). In the resulting dialog box, enter desired rotation. The choice to duplicate and rotate can be made here. The object above has been duplicated and rotated.

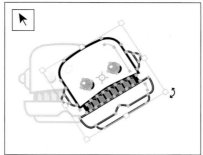

Rotate with the bounding box.
As the pointer reaches a certain distance from a bounding box, different cursors appear. Shown above is the rotate cursor. Click and drag in an arc to rotate freely.

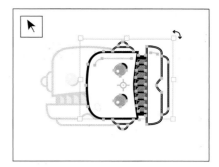

Rotate and constrain.
Rotate and hold the Shift key to constrain rotation to increments of 45 degrees.

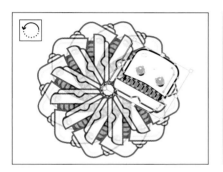

Transform again.
The last completed transform can be repeated by selecting Transform > Transform Again from the Object Menu. The rotate and duplicate transform was duplicated repeatedly for this figure.

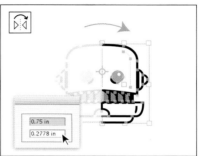

Reflect.
The reflect tool flips a selection across a virtual axis. Click once to set the origin and choose or enter the angle of reflection in the dialog.

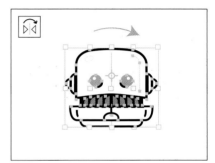

Choosing Copy in the dialog will flip a mirror image of the selection. This is a routine approach to drawing a complex symmetrical object. A reflection can be performed along any axis.

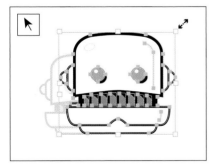

Scale.
To scale and maintain proportions, click a corner of the bounding box or click with the scale tool to set an origin for the selection. Hold down the Shift key and drag.

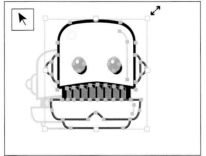

To scale without maintaining proportions, click a corner of the bounding box or click with the scale tool, and drag.

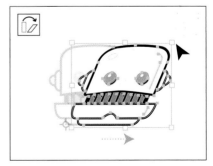

Shear or skew.
To skew a selection, click with the tool and drag. The tool can be constrained by axis and angle of shear or skew.

Tutorial:
Telemetry

The data relating to 2D spatial relationships, such as position, proximity, and dimension, can be collected, retrieved, and altered. This is critical to the precision of vector drawing and a feature that is often less exact in bitmap applications.

Alignment, distribution, and absolute point-level positioning are hallmarks of technical and informational graphics and for designing type. This exactitude is also necessary for motion applications where smooth transitions from frame to frame are essential. The typical tools found in many programs are demonstrated here.

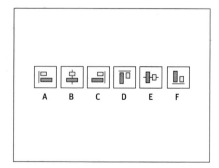

Align.
A. Align left.
B. Horizontal align center.
C. Align right.
D. Align top.
E. Vertical align center.
F. Align bottom.

Distribute.
A. Vertical distribute top.
B. Vertical distribute center.
C. Vertical distribute bottom.
D. Horizontal distribute left.
E. Horizontal distribute center.
F. Horizontal distribute right.

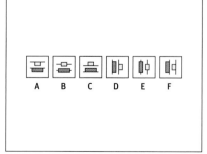

Guides and snap.
Grids and guides aid in positioning objects relative to the artboard and to each other. A "snap" function causes points and paths to jump into position, allowing absolute precision. In the figure above, the square has snapped left to a guide and the circle's bottom left anchor point has been snapped to the square's top left anchor point (shown as a red square).

38

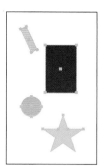

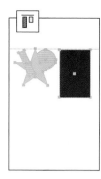
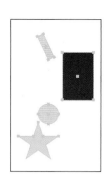
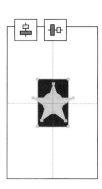

Alignment options.

Left: Select a series of objects and click the align left icon in the Align palette. The objects align to the farthest left object's outermost edge. Bounding boxes have been left out for clarity.

Top: Select a series of objects and click align top. The objects align to the farthest top object's uppermost edge.

Vertical and horizontal centers: Select a series of objects and click horizontal align center. Immediately click vertical align center. The objects center both directions to each other, not necessarily to the artboard.

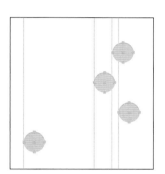
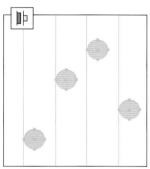
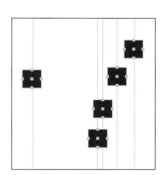
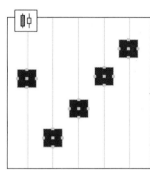

Distribution options.

Left: Distribution evenly spaces the far right and far left selected objects based on the distribution setting chosen. Select a set of objects and click on the horizontal distribute left icon in the Distribute Objects section of the Align palette. Objects distribute evenly against their left edges.

Center: Select a set of objects and click on the horizontal distribute left icon. Objects distribute based on the exact centers of each object.

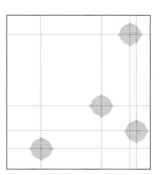
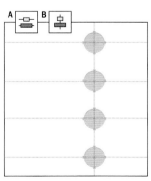
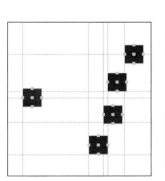
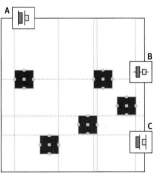

Alignment and distribution combinations.

Strategic combinations of distribution and alignment can aid dramatically in precise positioning.
A. Distribute centers horizontally.
B. Align horizontal centers.

A. Distribute all objects left horizontally.
B. Align vertical centers of top two squares.
C. Distribute bottom three objects left horizontally.

Tutorial:
The Mainspring

At the heart of a clearly defined 2D drawing environment is the constant aspect of a distinct and separate 3D space or stacking relationship between lines, shapes, and objects. The user benefits from the creative potential of objects as they overlap, touch, and obscure other shapes.

Although the concept of depth, background, and foreground is also implemented in bitmap applications and vector programs as layers, only vectors can remain on the same layer and maintain individual integrity. Interesting opportunities present themselves when stacking objects. An understanding of background, middle ground, and foreground attributes is the essence of the "Pathfinder" tools. With these tools, one shape is used to alter the appearance of another. These methods are explored on pages 38 and 39.

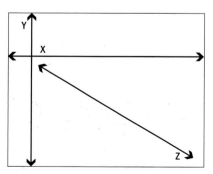

Objects in space.
Think of the artboard as a dimensional window. Objects occupy horizontal and vertical positions in space, as we have seen, but they also exist in "z" space. In these figures, bounding boxes are eliminated for illustrative purposes.

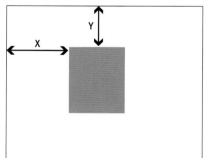

The position of objects in 2D space can be set visually or precisely using techniques already discussed. The z-space is the position of an object in space from front to back in a single layer. This is stacking.

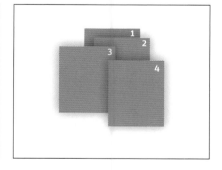

As soon as an object is added to the artboard, it occupies a position in z-space. The first object becomes the backmost object. As new elements are added, they stack from back to front.

40

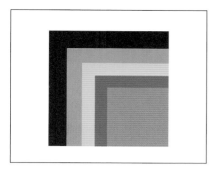

Object stacking.
This group of squares has been drawn one on top of another. The red square is the farthest background object. The blue square is the foreground object. Stacking objects can have dramatic impact on other functions.

Changing position of objects in a stack.
Position can be changed using a series of menu commands under Object > Arrange: Bring to Front, Send to Back, Bring Forward, and Send Backward. The red square has been brought to the front, covering up all other objects.

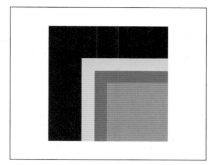

Bring Forward moves an object forward in a stack one step at a time. Here, the red square has been brought forward once.

Send to Back sends a selection behind all other objects. The green square has been sent to back.

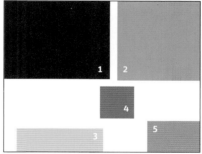

Objects that are not overlapping still maintain a stacking order.

Moving objects side to side, top to bottom does not affect the stacking order.

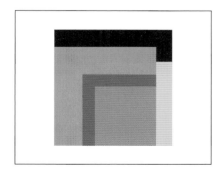

The yellow square is selected and sent backward once. This places it behind the orange square.

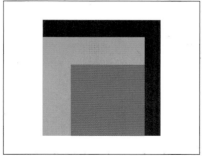

Multiple objects can be restacked as well. Here, the blue square and yellow square were selected simultaneously and sent to back.

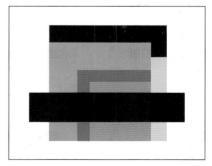

The purple rectangle is added. It becomes the frontmost object regardless of changes to the stacking order of the initial objects.

Artist profile:
Birgit Amadori

Country of origin: Germany
(now living in USA)

Primary software: Adobe® Illustrator®

Primary fields: Advertising, book cover
illustration, fine art, web

URLs: amadori.org, breastfeeding-art.com

Born in Frankfurt, Germany, Birgit Amadori received a Master's degree in Visual Communication from the University of Art, Offenbach. She now lives and works as a freelance illustrator in Redondo Beach, California, where she recently created cover illustrations for a series of Jane Austen novels published by Random House. Her other clients, both present and past, include Ogilvy & Mather Worldwide, Die Gestalten Verlag, Virgin Atlantic, Volkswagen, and Yahoo, although she finds creating original art for exhibition more fulfilling than work-for-hire projects.

Amadori has developed two distinctive vector styles using Adobe Illustrator CS1, both displaying her love of patterned elements. One is inspired by the complexity and detail of Art Nouveau, while the other employs more simplified faces, figures, and backgrounds. Says Amadori, "I love the cleanliness of vector art—even colors and straight, smooth lines—even in a very detailed image." All the images shown on this spread were created in Adobe Illustrator CS1.

As a longtime student of Asian and Japanese culture, Amadori created a series of cards for exhibition based on a traditional Japanese card game called Hanafuda ("Flower Cards"). She first discovered the game while reading the novel *Snakes and Earrings* by Hitomi Kanehara, started playing, and soon became fascinated by the artwork associated with the game. In Hanafuda, there are twelve suits of four cards each. The goal is to collect certain combinations, which earn you points. The person with the highest number of points wins. Each of the twelve suits has a single flower as its theme. For her designs, Amadori chose to introduce images of women along with the flower images.

1

2

An interesting aspect of Amadori's creative process is that she produces "originals" for exhibition using an embroidery technique. "I have the image printed without patterns on nylon cloth," she says. "Then I digitize just the square patterns so that my sewing machine can read it via a card reader. The machine then embroiders the square patches. When they are done, they are applied to the cloth in the same way as if they had been part of the artwork in Adobe Illustrator (so they're a tiled pattern). I do this because many galleries stubbornly refuse digitally created artworks because they are not originals. In this way, I can keep my style, but still produce originals to be exhibited."

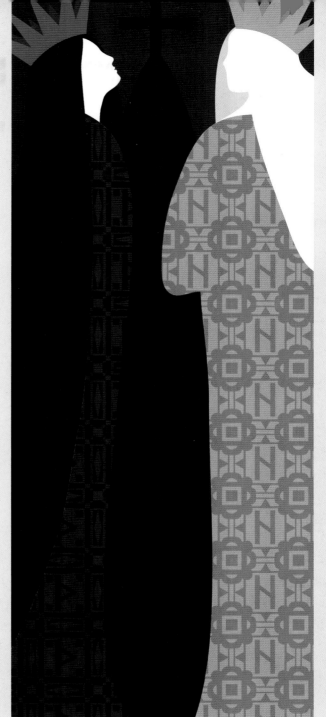

3

1. Kiku (Chrysanthemum) image from the artist's Hanafuda series. Printed on nylon with embroidery.
2. Brynhild: From breastfeeding-art.com, featuring goddesses and their babies.
3. Queens: Image from a series based on a Germanic folktale. Printed on nylon with embroidery.

All images © 2007 Birgit Amadori.

Artist profile:
Jon Burgerman

Country of origin: UK

Primary software: Adobe® Illustrator®

Primary fields: Wide range of media

URLs: jonburgerman.com, biro-web.com

A resident of Nottingham, UK, Jon Burgerman is known for his unique and colorful artwork in the fields of drawing, painting, print illustration, animation, street art, and toy design. He notes a sense of self-deprecation, humor, and anxiety in his work, which has been widely exhibited and published.

Over the years, Burgerman's characters and art have adorned bags, books, belts, snowboards, skateboards, surfboards, lunchboxes, stickers, posters, collectible toys, computer games, exhibitions, cell phones, clothing, cushions, mugs, wrapping paper, record covers, and frisbees. His client list includes the BBC, Sony, MTV, Pepsi, and Coca-Cola, among other high-profile organizations.

1

2

44

Burgerman has successfully combined his hand-drawn aesthetic with his vector work and describes his style as "swooping, rhyming lines interjected with strong colors and hyper-emotional characters." He does not trace over his lines with the pathfinder tool as many other artists do, and so he finds it important to "get the drawing and composition right" from early on. "Once the image is a vector shape," he says, "I will generally color it in, rescale, tweak, fiddle, move, move back again, until the composition is completed or until I just can't take working on it anymore."

Recently, Burgerman was commissioned, through the agency Cactus, to create artwork for a "pimped-out" ice-cream truck used by Own Your C—an anti–children smoking charity based in Colorado. "I was asked to give the truck some urban flair and youthful exuberance," he says. The final scanned and vectorized images were printed on a special vinyl and applied to the truck in Colorado.

3

4

1. Wrapping paper design for Nineteenseventythree (Brighton, UK).
2 & 4. Art and final product for Own Your C ice-cream truck for Cactus (Denver, Colorado).
3. Print advertisement for Sony PSP game Wipeout Pure.

All images © 2007 Jon Burgerman.

Iker Ayestarán

Country of origin: Spain

Primary software: FreeHand, Adobe® Photoshop®

Primary fields: Press, advertising, editorial, graphic design

URL: ikerayestaran.com

Iker Ayestarán studied graphic design at the school of arts in San Sebastián, Guipúzcoa, Spain, and photography at the Amaiur school. As an illustrator, editor, and graphic designer, he has worked for the newspapers *El Correo*, *Diario Publico*, and *Eroski*, for the magazines *Man*, *Mia*, and *Visual*, and for corporate publications for Prosegur, Bankinter, Telefónica, and other clients. He has also provided covers and illustrations for various books and published the book *Hidden Geometry* through the publishing house Blur Ediciones (2004).

Ayestarán generally starts with a pencil sketch, which he vectorizes in FreeHand and finally exports to Adobe Photoshop, where he gives it the final touches. "I prefer working with FreeHand, as it gives me freedom in composing my illustrations and realizing changes where and when necessary," he says.

His sources of inspiration are diverse: comics, graphics, photography. "I really like the French modern posters, the graphics from 1950s jazz record covers, Miroslav Sasek, and Saul Bass," he says.

While Ayestarán can work in various styles of illustration, he says he believes there are certain graphic and geometrical components that characterize his style. "In the case of publicity agencies, the work comes with a very defined concept and aesthetics, which implies that your style will be less implicit."

1

1. Thoughtful: Illustration for El Correo newspaper.
2. The Fall: Illustration for exhibition at Garabat Gallery Store.
3. Walk: Illustration for exhibition at Garabat Gallery Store.

   All images © 2007 Iker Ayestarán.

The apparent simplicity of the work belies the great sophistication of the illustrations. The beautiful use of FreeHand to create the basic structure and gesture of the figures—with clean lines and gentle, graceful curves— demonstrates the use of vectors at its best.

In many of Ayestarán's illustrations, solid areas of color border one another to define recognizable forms without the use of outlines and without the ubiquitous Illustrator gradients. In others, solid colors define basic shapes and linear elements lie on top, creating deceptively simple details.

2

3

Artist Profile: Iker Ayestarán

Engineering

3

Tutorial:
Gauges, Switches, and Dials

**As the design process progresses, the
need for more complex shapes grows
dramatically. Because the Pen tool can
be daunting at first, it is often preferable
to build new objects by combining
or deleting pieces of simpler shapes.**

One of the more powerful features in these applications is the
ability to cut, add, trim, and crop shapes. Referred to here as
Pathfinder tools (Adobe Illustrator nomenclature), they have
other names in different applications, but they all perform
similarly. Bitmap applications can perform similar functions,
but not with the precision and efficiency of a vector. This
is advantageous for reducing complexity. As you progress,
adding advanced features such as transparency and print
production will rely on stacking and pathfinder knowledge.

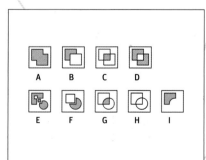

The Pathfinder tools.
A. Combine.
B. Minus front.
C. Intersect.
D. Exclude.
E. Divide.
F. Trim.
G. Crop.
H. Outline.
I. Minus back.

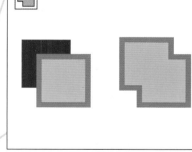

Combine or Add.
Combine selected shapes into one shape. New
object maintains the fill and stroke settings (the
appearance) of the top object.

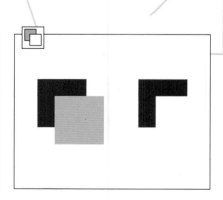

Minus Front.
Front object is subtracted from back object
where the objects overlap. New shape maintains
appearance of the back object.

50

Minus Front with stacked objects.
The yellow square is subtracted from the red square.
New shape maintains relative stacking position of
the selected objects.

Intersect or overlap.
The yellow square on the right is the result of an
intersect function. Only the areas of overlap remain,
with the appearance of the original top object.

 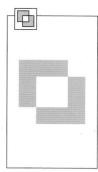

Exclude.
The inverse of Intersect. The area of overlap
is deleted.

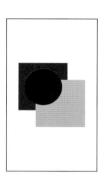 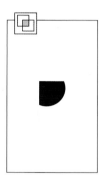

Intersect with stacked objects.
Three objects are selected. The Intersect command
is applied. The result is an object from the area of
overlap among all three.

Divide.
The Divide command splits the objects along all of
the areas of overlap, creating a jigsaw puzzle effect.
All original appearance attributes are maintained.

Trim.
Similar to subtract from front, Trim creates three
distinct objects, "trimming" the areas of overlap
and maintaining all appearance settings.

**Other Pathfinder
options.**
The original set
of shapes.

Crop.
Resembles a multiple
Intersect command.
The new shape retains
the source objects'
appearance.

Outline.
Outline does just
that, while dividing
the outlines into
separate segments.

Minus Back.
The red rectangle and
the star is chosen.
Minus Back is applied.
Minus Back is applied
again to the orange
rectangle and circle.

Pathfinder at work.
Each of the objects in the figures above uses
a default star primitive as a starting point.
They have been modified using a series of
simple Pathfinder functions. Try recreating them.

Switching Gears

There are alternative approaches to using the pathfinder toolbox for combining and deleting shapes. These can offer the user the opportunity for almost infinite exploration of design options before committing to a final design.

So far, the examples of the Pathfinder tools have shown "destructive" edits. This indicates that changes made during the design process are permanent. The option to utilize "nondestructive" edits is available as well. As the Pathfinder tools are applied, they are left fully editable and impermanent. Additionally, the Compound Path menu item is a cousin of the Pathfinder. It is used to create Pathfinder-like effects while retaining full editability of the resulting object. The downside of nondestructive edits is that they require more RAM and computer resources to maintain editability.

Many applications offer similar implementations. In most 3D applications, for example, there is a feature that allows for combining and subtracting 3D shapes (called Boolean operations). While the newly created shape is a combination of the original two, it has an invisible "history" that can be accessed to revise the shape at will or even return it to its original state.

The Compound Path.
Technically speaking, any object that overlaps another and appears to cut a "hole" is a Compound Path. A good example of a Compound Path is the letter "a." The center is cut out to form the counterspace of the letterform. The Pathfinder tools often form Compound Paths. The series above, however, is created manually by selecting all and choosing the Object > Compound Path menu. This creates an object that alternates between negative and positive shapes in areas of overlap.

This edit is also referred to as "nondestructive." The change is not permanent and each shape can be transformed independently of the others. The star is moved in 3 and rotated in 4. In 5 the corners of the square are selected with the direct-select tool and moved. In 6, color is added to each shape. The result is an object that maintains full editability. There are occasions when Compound Paths are used inherently and require specific knowledge of them, particularly in outlined type.

     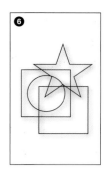

Pathfinder and nondestructive edits.

The figures above use a series of nondestructible (impermanent) Pathfinder commands. Figure 2 uses Minus Front to create the hole in the red square. In 3, Exclude is applied to the red and orange squares. Finally, 4 is the result of another Exclude.

Release Compound.

Applying the Release Compound option four times steps the object back through the edits to its original state in 5. In 6, the art has been returned to its basic primitive state.

Expanding or committing Pathfinder or Compound Paths.

Once a design is finished, the changes and edits can be "expanded." The edits become destructive, or permanent. It is always a good idea to save a copy of the live, editable art to accommodate inspiration or revision.

The series above represents a series of edits that include the use of multiple Transforms (Rotate, Skew, Scale), Merge, Crop, and Exclude Pathfinder operations and manipulations of directly selected points. It combines many of the techniques covered so far.

When first applied to the artboard, type is considered live and editable.

The Create Outline menu item creates a shape from the text. It is no longer editable as text.

Type > Release Compound Path and Object > Ungroup creates two shapes.

Now fully editable as a shape, any technique can be employed to modify the art. Logos often start this way.

As outlines, type can be transformed or manipulated like any shape.

Make Compound Path can return a letterform to an outline.

Tutorial:
Recalibration

Hand in hand with shapes, paths and strokes also offer opportunities for advanced design. The nature of constructing vector objects opens the door to potentially evolving simple paths and strokes into more interesting illustrative solutions.

Paths and strokes are not limited to simple lines around shapes. They provide a multitude of choices that yield additional methods for shape creation and transformation. Even the humble point can be useful for conjuring new and imaginative shapes.

Using the gamut of techniques touched on so far, and some new choices, the path can take on a life of its own.

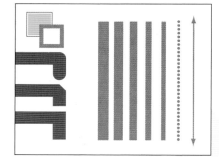

Strokes.
Paths have other unique properties that can be exploited to enhance creative opportunities with vectors. The width of a stroke can be set, its color changed, and style set to a dashed line. The endpoints and corners can be controlled and arrows added to either or both ends.

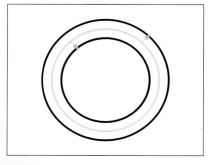

Offset Path.
A path can be offset with Object > Path > Outline Stroke. This is the surest way to create perfectly concentric circles—although it works on any path. The example shows the initial path (gray) offset a positive distance out and a negative distance toward center.

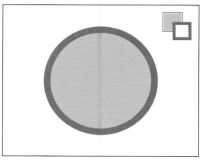

Stroke Path.
The path that defines an object can be stroked using attributes set in the color well, usually an icon of a solid square and an overlapping outline of a square. These are used to define and display the color and fill of an object.

54

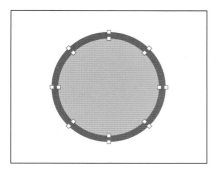

Outline Stroke.
The object is selected and Object > Path > Outline Path is chosen from the menu. The path has become an editable shape (and a compound path).

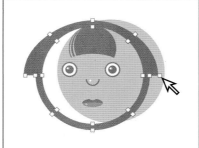

A fully editable shape.
The shape can be edited with any transformation tool. Outlining strokes is an extremely useful tool as a basis for more complex objects.

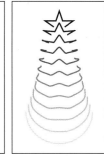

Blending.
Paths and shapes can be "blended" or morphed, changing color and shape over a user-specified number of steps or to create a smooth blend similar to an airbrush effect. This technique is used in Flash to create in-betweens—intermediate shapes that help create the illusion of movement.

Shapes on a path.
A series of blended shapes (the stars) can be attached to a path or a "spine."

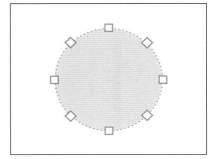

Default anchor points.
A primitive or regular shape has a default number of anchor points at equal distances. User-defined shapes can have any number of points with irregular spacing between points.

Add anchor points.
Using the Object > Path > Add Anchor Points menu, any path can have additional points added automatically to a path. They are positioned equally between each of the existing points.

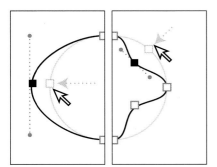

Manipulating anchor points.
Manipulating anchor points by direct-selecting them has been touched on previously. Adding more anchor points to a shape offers even more points for editing, without the need to draw them manually.

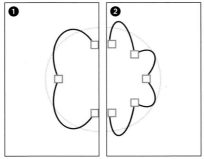

Distort and transform.
A more specialized set of distort and transform options can be found under Effect > Distort and Transform. There are a variety of tools available. Figure 2 is the result of a distort function applied to the objects from 1.

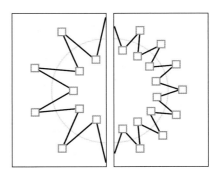

Anchor points and distort.
Here, more anchor points have been added and a distortion effect applied. Such changes can be used to create a dramatic effect on paths with different numbers of anchor points.

Tutorial:
A Stroke of Genius

Strokes offer greater utility as the user's command of the software improves. Vectors, all path-based, make lines and strokes the real building blocks by definition. Stroked paths are infinitely malleable. They can become shapes, be filtered, connected, reshaped, and changed to guides.

To some degree, an artificial distinction has been made between paths, strokes, shapes, and objects. The vocabulary is somewhat arbitrary, but can be simplified in this way: lines and paths are essentially the same thing (a subtle distinction is that paths tend to refer to closed objects, while lines are associated with unclosed objects) and stroked paths or lines have had, at minimum, a thickness and an end- or corner point defined.

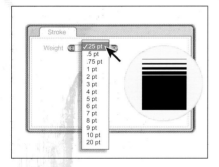

Setting Strokes.
Setting the width of a stroke is done by selecting the path and clicking on the weight dropdown to select the desired setting. The current color in the stroke color well is applied. If the color well is set to none, the path is stroked with black. The inset illustrates the results of various settings.

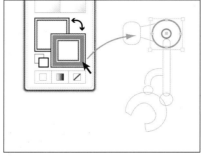

The stroke color well.
A single click on the stroke color well makes the stroke color option active. Any color swatch chosen will be selected in the well and applied to the stroke. To reactivate the fill color well click on it, and it will sit on top of the path well. Double clicking either well will invoke the traditional color picker.

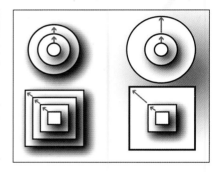

Offset Path vs multiple transforms.
The Offset Path command creates perfectly spaced offsets (the method for perfect concentric circles: A). Enlarging the object and using multiple, repeated transformations (Object > Transform > Transform Again) will not produce the same effect (B).

Outline Stroke.
The object is selected and Object > Path > Outline Path is chosen from the menu. The path has become an editable shape (and a compound path).

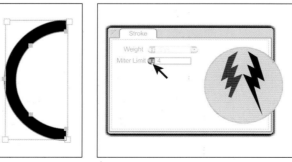

The miter limit.
The miter limit is a unique vector feature in drawing programs. It controls the shape of a pointed corner. A low miter limit setting results in a beveled corner: the red shape above. Higher limits result in pointed corners: the blue shape above. The miter limit applies strictly to strokes.

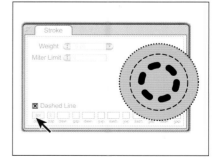

Dashed lines.
Any stroked path can be a dashed line. By selecting the stroked shape, clicking the check box, and entering values for the dash and gap size in points, the user can control a dashed stroke.

56

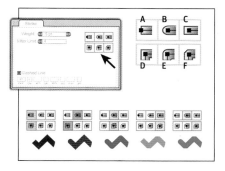
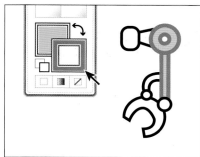
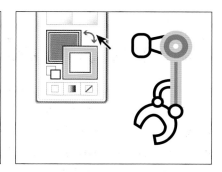

Setting end- and corner-point styles.
With a stroke selected, clicking on an icon for the corner or endpoint style will apply that style to the stroke. Any two end- and corner-point styles can be combined. A. Square endpoint. B. Rounded end. C. Square end, extends beyond endpoint. D. Square corner. E. Curved corner. F. Beveled corner.

Apply stroke color.
With a path selected, click on the stroke box in the color well. This applies the current color to the selected stroke.

Swap fill and stroke colors.
With a stroked and filled object selected, clicking on the arrow to the right of the color wells reverses the current color attributes. The stroke will become the fill and the fill will become the stroke.

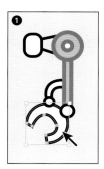

Sampling colors with Eyedropper.
Select an object (1). With the eyedropper click on an object that has the desired color styles. Those styles will be applied to the current selection, replacing the color attributes of the selection (2). Any number of objects can be selected for this color application method.

The Paint Bucket.
The paint bucket tool can be used to fill an object with the current color styles. This saves the step of selecting objects to apply the current style (2). The paint bucket can be used to apply the style to any number of objects by simply clicking on them.

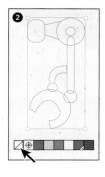

Drag and drop.
Similarly, the pointer tool can be used to drag a color from the swatches palette and drop it on an object without a selection (1). In 2, the "none" attribute has been applied to a selection of the entire set of objects. The "none" swatch is the square with the red slash across it.

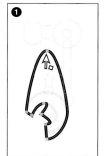

Manipulating anchor points.
Manipulating anchor points by direct-selecting them has been touched on previously. Adding more anchor points to a shape offers even more points for editing, without the need to draw them manually. They are added centered between each of the current anchor points (2: new points in red).

Distort and transform.
The significant transformation tools are available in the Object, Filter, and Effect menus in addition to the Toolbox. Figure 1 is the result of a Shear effect applied to all of the anchor points in the previous example. Figure 2 is the result of applying exactly the same effect with only two points (highlighted in red) selected.

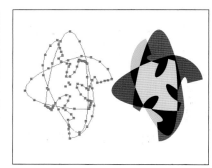

Simple transforms can yield interesting results.
Add Anchor Points was performed three times. Using a simple, often overlooked tool, (Transform each), a set of transformations (disproportionate scale, shear, move, and rotate) were performed simultaneously. The shapes were filled and set to Difference in the Transparency Palette. These techniques can offer dramatic results, with imaginative experimentation.

Tutorial:
The Bottom Line

The humble path is far more versatile than merely enclosing shapes. As the fundamental basis of vectors, paths originated with the most elementary choices for variation. The development of vectors has led to a myriad of options to evolve these simple building blocks into dramatic illustrative opportunities.

Strokes, in the most elementary sense, are simple lines around shapes, yet they can be the origin of more interesting shapes and can function as guides that determine the structure and shape of other objects (see the Art Brush). These choices provide methods for shape creation and transformation specific to paths. With its myriad options, the path is one of the most important vector tools, transcending the simple act of drawing.

Using the gamut of techniques touched on so far, and some new choices, the path can take on a life of its own.

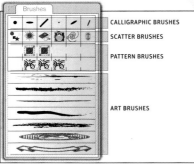

The Brushes palette.
The Brushes palette is the repository for all of the brush effects that can be applied to paths and strokes. To create a new brush of any type, just drag the art from the artboard.

Basic calligraphic brushes.
Calligraphic brushes mimic the effect of calligraphic pens, changing weight and thickness as the path changes direction.

The calligraphic brush and pressure sensitivity.
A pressure-sensitive tablet and stylus add a dimension to the calligraphic stroke that cannot be achieved with a mouse. Figure 1 is the result of mouse strokes; 2 demonstrates pressure sensitivity on the same stroke.

Applying new brush look to existing strokes.
Existing paths, shapes, and strokes can have a new brush look applied by selecting the path and clicking on the desired brush style in the Brushes palette.

Reshaping a brush stroke.
A brush stroke maintains its underlying stroke until it is made permanent. To reshape the path, direct-select an anchor point on the original path and drag or manipulate the direction points (1). The pencil can also be used by dragging it near a selected path (2). While not as accurate as the direct-selection method, it tends to create smoother curves.

Removing and Expanding a brush stroke.
In 1, the brush stroke has been removed with the Remove Brush Stroke menu item from the palette flyout menu. To expand a stroke (make it a shape instead of a stroke), choose Object > Expand Appearance, as shown in 2.

58

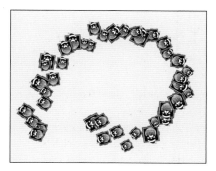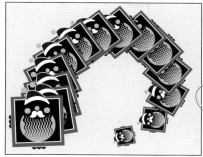

A scatter brush applied to a path.
A scatter brush is a brush created with a graphic and a set of user-defined variables. These variables can define rotation, size change, or orientation. With the Scatter Brush selected, draw a path and the path is painted with the graphic in a random scatter pattern.

A Scatter brush drawn with pressure sensitivity.
Pressure sensitivity adds a dimension to all of the brushes that isn't possible with a mouse. In this example, pressure controls the size, direction, spacing, and rotation of the brush relative to the 2D surface (the artboard).

In this example, the illusion of change in "3D" space, achieved by defining another pressure variable for the brush. Pressure changes the graphic relative to the path (imagined as a line in 3D space).

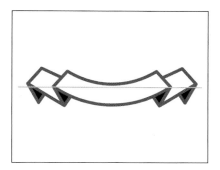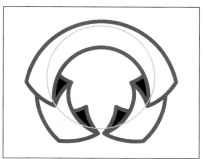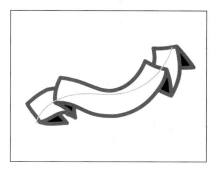

The art brush.
The art brush is also defined by a single graphic, but the underlying path (or spine) determines the shape of the graphic. The path acts as an armature that the graphic is mapped to. In this example, the path is a straight, horizontal line.

Interesting effects can be developed by using an art brush. Here, the same banner graphic is applied to a path that is a perfect circle.

This example uses a path that is a simple curve, creating an entirely different feel for the art than the other examples.

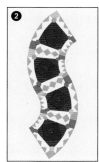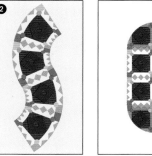

Pattern brushes.
A pattern brush is generally used to create borders. The user creates the graphics for inside corners, and outside corners, and sides, and defines the method that is used to apply the graphic as it turns corners or changes direction. In these examples, the brush is used to fill a shape (1) and to follow a path (2).

This is the more traditional use of the brush. Applied to a curved rectangle, it creates a simple decorative border. No corners were defined; the basic graphic is essentially chopped off to accommodate corners. This is achieved by making sure the size of the underlying path is an even multiple of the size of the pattern tile.

This graphic was originally created to demonstrate patterns. The original graphic was reused here to create a decorative border. A library of previously developed art can yield unexpected and satisfying results when reused as a brush.

 59

Tutorial:

Strata

Layers are found in almost every graphics application. Illustration, animation, painting, 3D, video, or layout programs—whether they are vector-based or not—will offer layers as a feature.

Layers became ubiquitous because they were such a brilliantly simple addition to software in general. The advantages of layers are obvious and because they are found in such a wide variety of application types, this section will act as a review of the basics of layers as they are implemented in most leading graphics software.

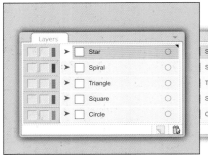

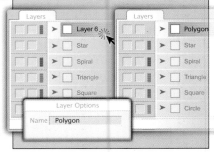

Layer palette.
The basic Layer palette. Allows for the management of layers through options for layering, hierarchy, visibility, and editability. The palette provides visual feedback indicating the current status of any object.

Creating a new layer.
Clicking on the new document icon creates a new layer. New layers are always created above the currently selected layer.

Renaming a layer.
New layers default to "Layer x," where "x" is the number after the last layer created. Double-clicking on the layer name will bring up a dialog, or offer some other method for naming a layer.

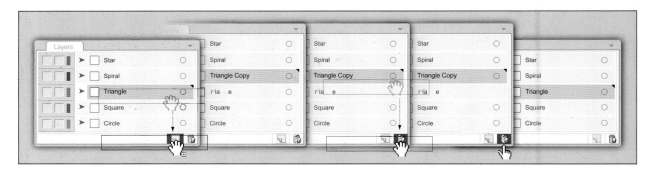

Duplicating a layer.
The easiest method for duplicating an existing layer is to drag the layer over the new document icon. This will create a layer with the default name of "layer name copy." The duplicate layer is created above the current layer.

Deleting a layer.
Deleting a layer is similar to adding one. Drag the layer over the trashcan in the layer palette. A warning dialog will confirm your decision to throw away the layer.

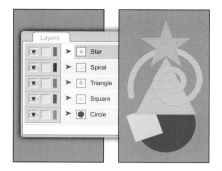

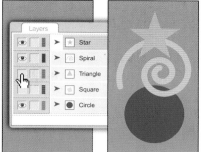

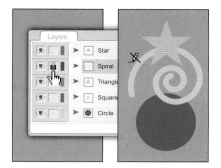

Visibility.
An eye on the left in a layer's info area indicates that a layer is currently visible.

Hiding a layer.
Clicking on the eye will hide the eye icon and make that layer invisible. Invisible layers can't be edited.

Locked layers.
Locked layers can't be edited. A locked layer can be either visible or hidden.

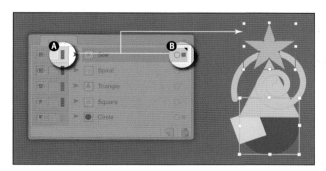

Object Selection color.
The color in the info area of the box (A). It also appears on the far right when objects are selected on that layer (B). This color is displayed to indicate selections, paths, points, and other layer-specific interface elements. These colors can be changed by the user.

Reorder layers.
Changing the order of a layer requires clicking and dragging the layer to a new position. Some visual cue (the double red lines in this example) will indicate that the layer can be "dropped" in the new location.

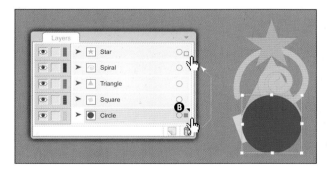

Moving a shape from one layer to another.
Clicking on the object selection indicator (B) and dragging in the palette from one layer to another will move the selected object.

Moving a copy of a shape from one layer to another.
Clicking on the object selection indicator (B) and Option/Alt dragging in the palette from one layer to another will move a copy of the selected object.

Tutorial:
Precision Tune

Vectors have been demonstrated as a precise medium for drawing. The alignment palette has been explored, but it has one drawback: the absolute positioning of objects relative to each other. The edge of a circle may align with the edge of a square, but they are not visually aligned. With grids, rulers, guides, and "snap" assistance, alignment can be further refined.

Vector

Bitmap

Like most graphics applications, vectors programs offer a variety of tools to guide in the process of creating precise relationships between objects. The one clear difference between a vector and a bitmap in alignment is the "fuzzy" or anti-aliased edge that figures into the alignment process with bitmaps. Precise alignment is not technically possible because of the extra pixels. Visual alignment is even more critical with bitmaps and is another difference between vectors and pixels. Whether or not the difference is critical depends on the job at hand.

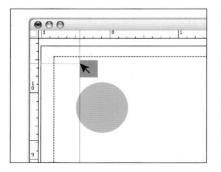

Cursor tracking and visual alignment.
Visual alignment requires compensating for irregular or organic shapes by adjusting the irregular or curved side to align with objects that have a more definitive edge for alignment. The circle is slightly to the left of the guide to create the perception of alignment. At the top and left, in the ruler area (the red lines in the insets) is a visual indicator that moves relative to the position of the tip of the cursor. This is another handy tool for positioning.

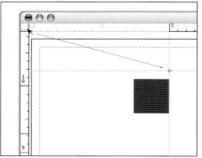

Zero point.
The upper left corner of the ruler can be dragged to any location on the artboard, allowing for easy visual and numerical positioning. The zero point can be reset to default by double-clicking the same area in the upper left of the ruler.

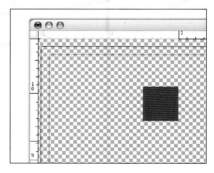

The transparency grid.
In order to recognize transparent areas within the art (rather than areas that are filled white), turn the transparency grid on. Areas that are "clear" are easily recognizable. This has many practical uses. Exporting art into other applications that support transparency is a common use. Transparency can aid in defining a text wrap in page layout or for common bitmap.

62

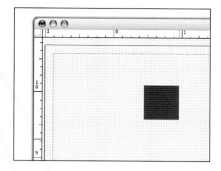

Grids.
Grids can be activated from the View menu. The attributes of the grid can be edited to suit any need. The space between lines, the color of the grid, or the grid's position in the stacking order (in back of all objects or in front) are examples of editable aspects of a grid.

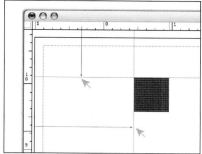

Ruler guides.
Ruler guides, one of the essential alignment tools, are accessed by clicking in the top ruler area or in the left and dragging to the desired location on the artboard.

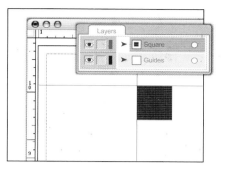

Guides and layers.
Guides are specific to a layer. Each layer can have its own set of guides, although this can be confusing. One solution is to place all guides on a single layer. This is an efficient way to turn all guides on or off, without the need to search for a guide through multiple layers.

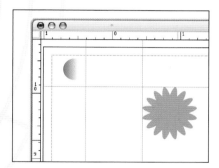

Alignment of objects to grid or guides.
The "Snap" options can be toggled on and off from the View menu. Snapping to a grid or a point forces a dragged object to snap into place as it approaches a grid division or a point. This forces precise alignment within defined parameters.

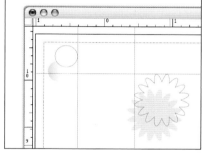

Creating a guide out of an object.
View > Guides > Make Guides will convert an object into a guide (the blue lines above represent converted objects). This technique can be beneficial in instances that require a unique relationship between two objects. One object is turned into a guide. The second object is positioned relative to the guide before releasing the first object.

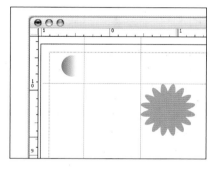

Release guides.
Guides can be edited, moved, or deleted by unlocking guides from the guides submenu. With guides unlocked, choose a guide (or multiple guides) and edit as necessary. To release a guide (particularly an object), choose the object and release. This returns the object to its pre-guide condition. Remember to lock guides again.

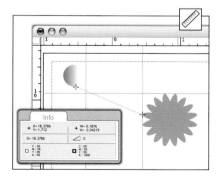

The Measure tool.
The Measure tool behaves exactly as expected. Working like a very precise ruler, click and drag from one point to another. The info palette reports the exact measurement. This is most effective when measurements are taken from specific, anchor, or curve points so that remeasurement is from a consistent set of points.

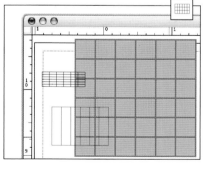

The rectangular grid.
The rectangular grid tool is more flexible than the global grid. The tool allows for any number of grids in any position. The grids can be stroked and filled, converted to guides or used to quickly create columns for text placement.

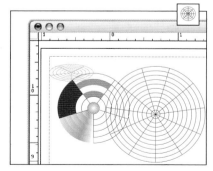

The polar grid.
The polar grid behaves in the same fashion as the rectangular grid and is especially useful for creating elliptical objects with equal subdivisions.

Tutorial:
Subsystems Check

Just as with any worthwhile endeavor, learning the basics of drawing with vector tools is absolutely essential. Whether drawing in an illustration application, creating a letterform, or drawing a sprite for animation, the basic skills are all the same. Mastery of these tools cross application boundaries.

If nothing else, expertly drawing with the pen tool will serve you well in any vector application. It is the heart and soul of the process. While difficult for some to master (as drawing this way is counterintuitive), it is well worth the time and effort necessary to become fluent and leverage this skill into other applications.

64

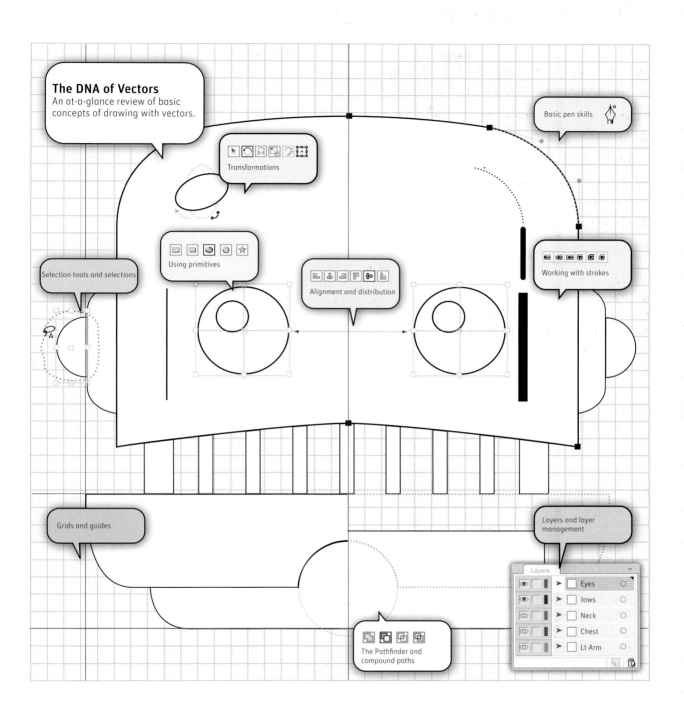

The DNA of Vectors
An at-a-glance review of basic concepts of drawing with vectors.

Basic pen skills

Transformations

Selection tools and selections

Using primitives

Alignment and distribution

Working with strokes

Grids and guides

Layers and layer management

The Pathfinder and compound paths

Layers

- Eyes
- Jaws
- Neck
- Chest
- Lt Arm

Artist profile:
Brad Hamann

Country of origin: USA

Primary software: Adobe® Illustrator®, Adobe® Photoshop®

Primary fields: Editorial, advertising

URL: bradhamann.com

Brad Hamann is a native New Yorker and a graduate of Parsons School of Design. His work has appeared in many of America's leading magazines and newspapers including *The New York Times* and *The Wall Street Journal*, as well as major advertising campaigns for Honda of America, Schick, and Calloway Golf, among other clients.

Hamann has taught traditional illustration at Parsons and now teaches digital illustration at Syracuse University and Marist College. He maintains a home and studio in Red Hook, New York, and is pursuing a Master's degree in graphic design at Marywood University.

1

2

When he made the switch from traditional methods (pen and ink, acrylics, and so on) to Adobe Illustrator back in 1993, he never looked back. "My hardline graphic style worked well as digital art, and I was able to execute more accurately what was in my head, while expanding and speeding up the production of art. It felt like coming home," he says.

Hamann lists among his artistic influences M.C. Escher, comics legend Jack Kirby, and children's book illustrators Leo and Diane Dillon. His work, which swings from humorous to comic book to Pop Art to more realistic styles, is notable for its complex paths and shapes, as well as its sophisticated use of clipping paths and masks.

Hamann's standard creative steps include collecting reference, doing pencil drawings to lay out the illustration, scanning the pencil drawings and rendering them in Adobe Illustrator, and then exporting them to Adobe Photoshop for "minor enhancement" if needed.

"Once I get my students to start using the pen tool and the pathfinder panel, I know we're on our way," he says. "Almost every one of them falls in love with Adobe Illustrator once I guide them through the early minefields that discourage most beginners. Then off they go!"

3

4

1. **Rage:** Personal piece. "Working with an older Illustrator file (the woman), I mixed textures and photo collage in Photoshop," says the artist.
2. **Fantastic Five:** Illustration for an article in *Diablo* magazine featuring socially conscious inventors and innovators.
3. **Summer Reading:** A large piece created for *The Hartford Courant*.
4. *The Real World Comes to Denver:* Comic strip–style telling of the production of the MTV television show in 2006, done for *The Denver Post*.

All images © 2007 Brad Hamann.

Artist profile:

Mar Hernández (aka Malota)

Country of origin: Spain

Primary software: Adobe® Photoshop®, FreeHand

Primary fields: Advertising, editorial, public relations, package design

URL: malotaprojects.com

Mar Hernández was born in Jaen, Spain, grew up in Yecla, and studied art and audiovisual work at San Carlos Fine Arts University. She now lives in Valencia, Spain, where she works as a freelance illustrator and designer. Her recent clients include MTV International, Cactus Island Recordings, *d[x]i* magazine, Armada Skis, and superinteressante mgz. Her artwork is distinguished by its elegant use of shape and figure–ground relationships and its lack of outlines.

1

2

Although she enjoys the speed and flexibility of digital art, Hernández notes one great disadvantage: "Digital art is not as well recognized as 'traditional' art. There are still a lot of people who prefer a hand-painted piece and underestimate the printed work; they don't realize that what matters is the message the work transmits."

Hernández prefers to work in simple forms, with restricted color schemes, adding complementary colors for visual rhythm. Her work also emphasizes rotational and axial (bilateral) symmetry. "When we constantly work at something," she says, "it's unavoidable that with time there are reiterative resources, forms, and colors—and it's this reiteration, with some extra variations, that defines an artistic style."

Hernández's creative process rarely varies: she first identifies what the customer wants; gathers references and studies similar projects; sketches out her ideas either on paper or by computer depending on the project; discusses the sketches with the client and revises them until they are approved; and draws the final piece in FreeHand. "When I'm happy with the result, I usually translate my drawing to Adobe Photoshop and fix some colors, gradients, and shapes. I also add some patterns and textures to finish my work," comments Hernández.

1. A lion character from the artist's contest-winning series of book covers.
2. Illustration for the Born to be Green exhibition, based on the character Treeson created by Bubi au Yeung in Taiwan and produced by Crazy Label (wookieweb.com/crazylabel).
3. The result of a collaboration between Hernández and designer, illustrator, paper engineer, and toymaker Carlo Giovani (carlogiovani.com).
4. Illustration using "hair" as a theme for d[x]i magazine.

All images © 2007 Mar Hernández.

4

3

Artist Profile: Mar Hernández (aka Malota)

Chisato Shinya (aka Kinpro)

Country of origin: Japan

Primary software: Adobe® Illustrator®

Primary fields: Magazine and book illustration, advertising, interior design, clothing design

URL: kin-pro.com

Born in Sapporo, Japan, where she still lives, Chisato Shinya graduated from the evening course at Hokkaido Institute of Design. She then worked at a design production company for three years before becoming a full-time freelancer at the age of 24. Her pseudonym, Kinpro, is short for Kin-taro (an old Japanese tale) and "professional."

2

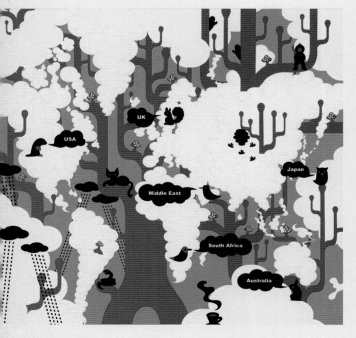

1

Among her many projects, Shinya once worked with a group of artists to redesign the Hotel Fox in Denmark, while her glasses and coasters have been released by ChilliChilly in Hong Kong. She contributed several illustrations to the book *Grimm*, a contemporary version of Grimm's Fairy Tales published by Die Gestalten Verlag in 2003. She has also designed a cover for the design webzine *Shift* (shift.jp.org) and has exhibited her work at art spaces around the world, including Sapporo's Soso Café and Barcelona's Maxalot Gallery.

"Even before I started using digital tools," says Shinya, "I always attempted to draw beautiful lines. This is what attracted me to vector art. It enables me to draw whatever I like, however I want." Her creative process begins with rough sketches and random scribbles drawn with a thin pen. "Ideas gradually become concrete," comments Shinya. She then completes the work in Adobe Illustrator.

3

4

Shinya prides herself on having a flexible style and continually challenges herself to progress and change as an artist. She is inspired by painting, photography, and music, and she lists Italian designer Bruno Munari and graphic artist Keiji Ito among her influences.

The natural environment and the human imagination are especially important in Shinya's work. "I would never be able to live somewhere where there are no trees," she says. The intricate forest patterns in her work, limned with simple contrasts, evoke the Japanese landscape she loves, and her compositions contain mysterious forms and unexpected objects that invite the viewer into the "story" of the images.

1. Contribution to *Designed to Help*, a book published by Die Gestalten Verlag for charities helping victims of the Sumatra tsunami.
2. Cover from the May 2007 issue of *Computer Arts* magazine.
3. Wallpaper artwork for "Maxalot Wallpaper Collection," a project by Maxalot, a gallery in Barcelona, Spain.
4. A work from the artist's first solo exhibition, Visible form/Invisible form.

All images © 2007 Chisato Shinya.

Aesthetics

4

Tutorial:
Color Codes

Most graphics applications offer the user many different color models to choose from. The final use of the art, usually for print or online, determines the color model that will be used for a project. RGB (red, green, blue) is the native color space of computers, and is generally used for web or online purposes. CMYK (cyan, magenta, yellow, and black) is strictly used for print.

Color theory and management are complex issues beyond the scope of this tutorial. However, a basic understanding of the different color models will provide the beginning user with the insight necessary to choose the correct model at the start of a project, eliminating potential problems as a project progresses.

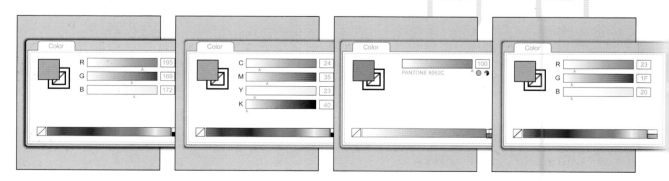

Color models: RGB.
The native color space of the computer and other light-emitting sources such as television, RGB creates far more colors than the human eye can perceive.

Color models: CMYK.
The CMYK color space is strictly used for offset printing. A series of tiny dots creates the illusion of full color. It represents a much smaller gamut (or range) of colors, a limitation that can create problems converting from RGB to CMYK.

Spot colors.
Spot colors are also specific to printing, but they are flat colors (not defined by dots) and are used in addition to CMYK. Chosen from specific libraries, such as Pantone Matching System (PMS) or Trumatch, they are specially mixed colors difficult to reproduce in CMYK or colors with specific properties such as metallic or fluorescent.

Color models: websafe.
Less and less relevant as the average computer users adopt better monitors, the web safe palette is a subset of RGB colors that were chosen to provide consistent color over a wider range of monitors.

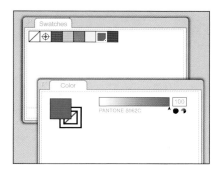

Swatch and color palettes.

The Swatch palette can contain any kind of swatch: CMYK colors, spot colors, patterns, or gradients. The color palette provides additional control over specific color attributes, particularly the color's value.

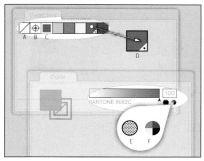

Swatch palette definitions.

A. Indicates "none" (no color applied).
B. Registration. Apply to objects that won't print.
C. Heavy white outline indicates selected color.
D. Spot colors. Indicated by triangle and dot.
E, F. Convert colors between RGB, Spot, and CMYK.

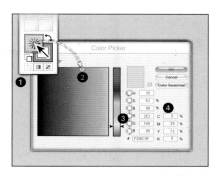

Editing colors.

Double-clicking either the fill or the stroke well in the tool palette (1) will invoke the color picker dialog. Colors can be chosen in the interactive color area by dragging the color target (2), using the color slider (3), or numerically (4).

Sampling colors.

Sampling colors is as simple as using the eyedropper to click on the desired color anywhere in the document. This places the color in the fill or stroke color well. If an object is selected when the eyedropper is used, the color sample will be applied to the object.

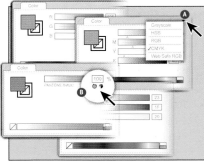

Drag and drop a color to the Swatches palette.

With the desired color in the color well (fill or stroke), click on the color in the well and drag and drop it on the Swatches palette. Double-click the swatch to enter a name for the color in the subsequent dialog box.

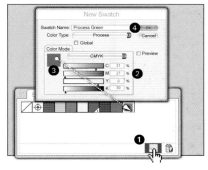

Creating new swatch from the Swatches palette.

Click on the document icon at the bottom of the palette (1). Numerically or using the sliders, define a color (2). A preview displays the color as you create it (3). Satisfied with the color, name it and click "OK" to add it to the palette (4).

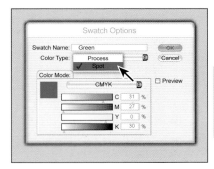

Converting any color to a spot color.

Double-click on a color in the swatch palette. In the resulting Swatch Options dialog, click on the Color Type dropdown menu. Choose Spot. This allows the use of a process color as if it were a spot (specifically to create tints). It can be converted back to process at any time.

Switching from one color mode to another.

There are various ways and different reasons to convert from one color model to another. Many applications offer flyout menus (A) for certain tasks. With a color selected, simply click on the menu indicator and choose a new color mode. In the color palette, the icons under the value indicator (B) also convert colors to RGB or CMYK.

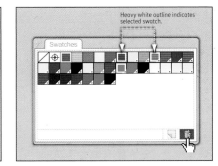

Delete unused colors.

The Swatch palette can often become crowded and unwieldy as work progresses. To delete a swatch, select it and click on the trash can icon, or drag it over the trash. Using the swatches palette flyout menu, the user can also delete all unused colors.

The Interpolator

Shape blends are a feature in vector applications that aren't found in their bitmap cousins. For instance, Adobe Flash uses shape blends to create the images required to "tween," or morph, between two key objects. This is essential to create the illusion of movement.

It is simpler and more efficient to create airbrush-like effects with gradients than shape blends, but shape blends allow the user to create these smooth blends in more organic shapes. Shape blends can also be used to evenly distribute a series of objects over a specific distance or to blend between two very different shapes. These blends must be used judiciously as they are very memory-intensive and can create large files.

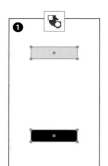 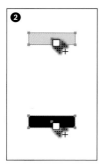  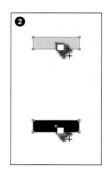  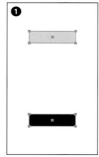

Creating a smooth blend.
1. Draw two rectangles spaced some distance apart.
2. Using the blend tool (shown at the top of 1), click on an anchor point on the first shape and then click on the same anchor point on the second shape.
3. A smooth blend will be created between the two objects.

Creating a blend with a specified number of steps.
1. Create two shapes.
2. Click on an anchor point on the first object and then Option/Alt click on the same anchor point in the second shape.
3. This will produce a dialog box that provides an input box to enter the number of in between shapes required. In this example, four steps were specified.

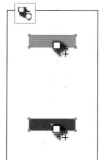   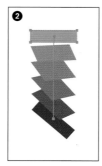 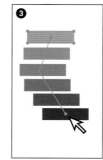 

Simple shape color blend.
Creating a color blend is identical to a blend in black and white, with one exception: the choice of colors has a significant impact on the blend and how it prints. Blending between a spot color and a process color will create a blend composed of process colors. Blending between two spot colors will create in between shapes in process colors, leaving the spot colors unchanged.

The live blend advantage.
When blends are created they are live, meaning changes can be made without reblending. Just changing the color of one of the source shapes will change the blended result (1). Either of the source shapes can be transformed and the blend will update to reflect the change. In 2, the bottom shape was rotated. This created not only a color blend, but a distinct shape blend as well. This live aspect also applies to the "spine" of the blend. The spine is a path that connects the two source shapes. The path can be modified like any other path (in 3 an anchor point was added) or the spine can be replaced completely with a new path (4).

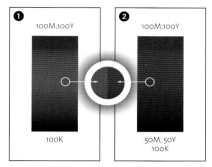
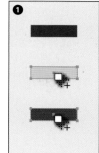

① 100M,100Y ... **100K**

② 100M,100Y ... **50M, 50Y 100K**

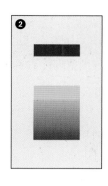  

Advanced color blends.
An important factor in creating a smooth color blend is making sure process colors are composed of CMYK mixes that share colors. In 1, black (100% K) is blended with red (100% M, 100% Y). As the red blends toward black, an undesirable "gray" area appears (see inset). In 2, black is a mix of magenta, yellow, and black (50% M, 50% Y, and 100% K). As the red (100% M, 100% Y) blends toward black, the extra color in the black eliminates the "gray" effect.

Multicolor blends.
Blends can be created out of multiple shapes and multiple colors. To create a blend from more than two shapes, create the first blend (1 and 2). Direct select the second and third shapes, and use the blend tool to blend again (3 and 4).

   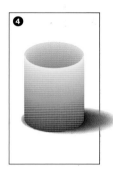

Blending paths.
Blends between paths are created using the same methods as shape blends. Paths can be blended in a user-specified number of steps, just like shapes, but with an altogether different effect.

The same set of paths blended with a smooth blend. In 1, the bottom path was also the top-most object, creating the lighter area at the bottom of the blend. In 2, the top path was brought to the front before blending. This creates the illusion of a "top" for the cylinder.

In 3, the ellipses were split apart and blended separately to create a front for the cylinder and an inside that darkens more as it recedes into the shape. In 4, two off-center elliptical paths were blended, a Feather filter was applied, and the blend was sent to back to create a shadow.

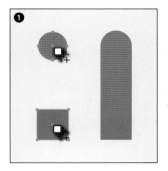 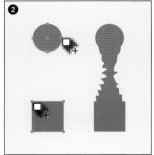

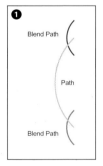 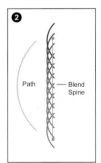 

Choosing beginning and endpoints.
In 1, two different shapes are being blended together. The blend is created from the same points on each shape and a smooth blend is created between shapes and colors. Choosing anchor points from different locations (2) produces dramatically different results. This technique can be used to great advantage and is another unique quality of vectors.

Replace the spine of a blend.
A well-planned and deliberate use of the Object > Blend > Replace Spine command opens up a broad area for the creative use of blends to create more organic shapes and effects. In 1, two paths are drawn for a blend, and a path is drawn that will be the final spine. In 2, the blend is created (its spine is a blue line in the center of the blend). In 3, the blend and the path are selected, and the Object > Blend > Replace Spine menu item is selected.

Tutorial:
Gradual Progress

Gradients are a mainstay of much of the contemporary illustration produced today. The ease with which an airbrush effect can be produced has encouraged designers and illustrators to use them extensively—at times even overuse them.

Gradients are extremely easy to create and apply, and can be used quite effectively to create volume and depth. They are limited to radial (circular) and linear styles, making them difficult to use in organic shapes. These two styles limit gradients by creating visible areas of demarcation between blended colors that may interfere with the contour of the shape.

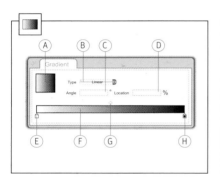

Default Gradient palette.
Gradient fill box (A); gradient type dropdown (B); angle of blend relative to shape (C); location of midpoint diamond (D); gradient slider, endpoint color, gradient color swatch (E); gradient bar (F); midpoint diamond (G); gradient slider, endpoint color, gradient color swatch (H).

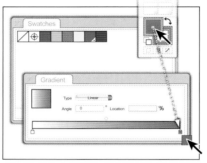

Create a simple two-color gradient.
Select a color and drag and drop it onto the far right gradient slider. Leave the far left gradient slider white. This is a simple two-color gradient (violet to white).

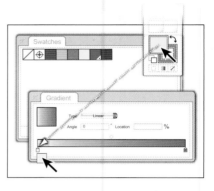

Modify a simple two-color gradient.
Select a second color and drag it to the far left gradient color square. This is a basic edit to a gradient. Selecting another color and dragging it to the same color square would replace the yellow with the new color, changing the gradient.

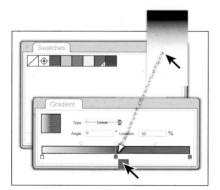

Create a gradient with multiple colors.
To add a third color to the gradient, select another color and drag it under the gradient bar. This will create a new color swatch in the selected color. Two new midpoint diamonds are created on either side of the new swatch. The midpoint diamond defaults to a position exactly halfway between two adjacent colors.

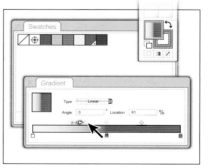

Move the midpoint in a gradient.
The midpoint is the point at which the transition between two colors begins (the default is 50%). By moving the leftmost midpoint to the right, the gradient starts sooner. This also results in more yellow in the blend than red. The Location input box will change to reflect the new position of the midpoint.

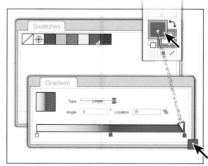

Edit the color in a gradient.
As indicated in the figure above, dragging a new color over a gradient square replaces the previous color and creates a new gradient.

78

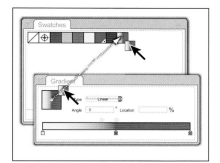

Saving a gradient.
To save a gradient for future use, drag the gradient from the gradient fill box and drop it into the Swatches palette. Neglecting to do this will cause the loss of the gradient when the next gradient is created.

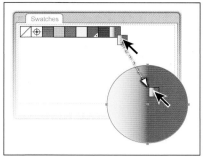

Applying a gradient to a shape.
Click on a gradient swatch and drag it over the shape to apply the color OR select the shape and click on the gradient in the Swatches palette. This creates a default linear gradient.

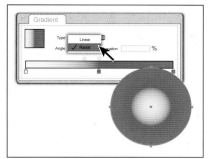

Changing the gradient type.
With the object still selected, click on the Type dropdown and choose "radial." This changes the gradient to a series of concentric colors that emanate out from a center point.

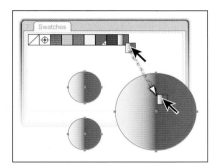

Applying a gradient to multiple shapes.
With the objects selected, click on the gradient swatch or drag and drop the swatch on one of the shapes. By default, this results in the gradient being applied to each object individually.

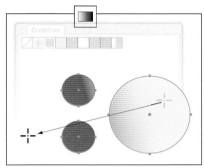

Applying a gradient to multiple shapes.
To reapply the gradient so that it colors the group as if it were a single shape, choose the gradient tool from the tool palette and click and drag across the shapes. This can be done from any position or direction to achieve different results.

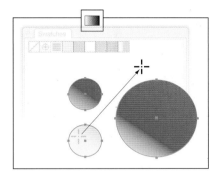

Changing the angle of the gradient.
The angle of the gradient can be changed by entering a number into the Angle input box or interactively by clicking and dragging across the selected shapes. The interactive approach is more intuitive, but less precise.

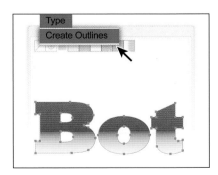

Applying a gradient to type.
To apply a gradient to type, outline the text and then follow the standard gradient processes.

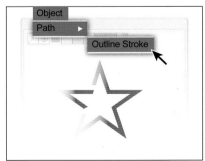

Applying a gradient to a path.
Select the path and outline the stroke. Use the standard gradient method to apply a gradient. When converting text to outlines or outlining a stroke, it's a good idea to save copies of the original text and path on a different layer—just in case.

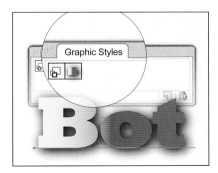

Applying a gradient to live type.
A little-known technique will allow a user to create an appearance that contains the gradient and defines it as a new graphic style. The graphic style can then be applied to text without outlining it, keeping the text live and editable. (Appearances are covered on pages 86 and 87.)

Tutorial:
How to Make a Mesh

The concept of the gradient mesh is a nod toward making vectors behave a bit more like bitmaps. It provides a tool that allows for the creation of organic blends—blends that can move in different directions with smooth transitions. This can be considered "painting" with vectors.

Simple gradients are limited to linear and radial blends. The transitions always occur in the same direction, but they are light on system resources. Shape blends offer more freedom and can be used in ways that don't appear as linear, although they still tend to have hard edges and can quickly become large and potentially unprintable. The gradient mesh offers the ultimate freedom in color blending, but it can soon consume RAM and increase file sizes. Creating multiple meshes, rather than a single large mesh, is the ideal use of the tool. However, experience is the ingredient necessary to make the decision to use one method over another.

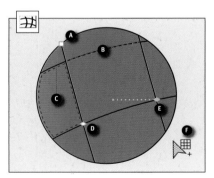

Anatomy of a mesh (extreme closeup).
A. Anchor point
B. Mesh line
C. Mesh patch
D. Unselected mesh point (diamond shape)
E. Selected mesh point with direction line
F. Mesh tool cursor

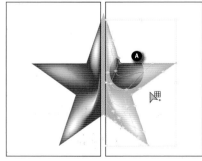

Using the mesh tool.
Clicking on a shape with the mesh tool creates a mesh. A mesh cannot be created from compound paths or text objects (live text). Using the mesh tool is less desirable for more complex objects.

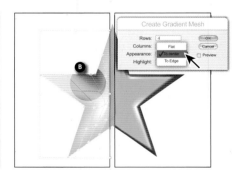

The Create Gradient Mesh command.
Selecting a shape and choosing Object > Create Gradient Mesh provides access to a dialog box to input mesh characteristics and creates a much more precise mesh. Compare the mesh points created in A with those created in B.

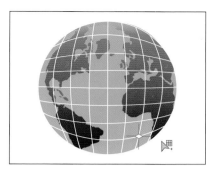

Selecting a mesh point.
Create a mesh using Create Gradient Mesh command, eight columns and eight rows, flat, no highlight. (Some interface elements have been simplified or eliminated for clarity: the white lines represent the mesh.) A point has been selected with the mesh tool.

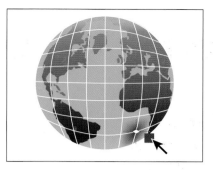

Adding color to a mesh point.
With the mesh point selected, drag and drop a color onto the selected point. This adds color from the point out.

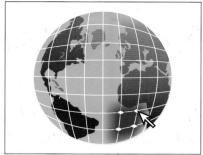

Adding color to multiple mesh points.
The direct-selection tool can also be used to select points. With four points selected, a color has been dragged over any of the points.

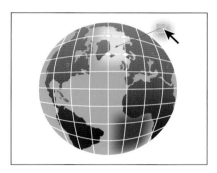

Adding color to a mesh patch.
Click on a patch (a region surrounded by mesh lines) with the direct-selection tool and drag a color over the patch.

Adding color to multiple mesh patches.
With the direct-selection tool, shift-click on a series of patches. Drag and drop a color swatch over each patch. Adding a color to multiple mesh patches. With the direct-selection tool, shift-click on a series of patches. Drag and drop a color swatch over each patch.

Adding a mesh point to a mesh patch.
Using the mesh tool, click on a patch area (not on the edge or on another point) to create another set of mesh points and patches. Two lines will be created perpendicular to each other.

Deleting a mesh point.
Using the mesh tool, Option/Alt click on a mesh point with the mesh tool. This will delete the point and the corresponding mesh lines.

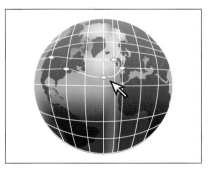

Adjusting the position of a mesh point.
Direct-select mesh points (shift-click to select multiple points). Drag the points to a new location. Points can also be moved with the mesh tool. Be careful to click on a point.

Adjusting the direction of a mesh point.
Mesh direction lines are moved like direction lines on ordinary anchor points. The result, though, is a change in the angle and direction of the blends.

Revealing Masks

Clipping paths and opacity masks are techniques used to crop or hide art. Clipping paths are used extensively in the process of creating art in such applications as Adobe Illustrator and are a method unique to vector programs. Opacity masks (or alpha channels) can be found in most pixel-based applications, but are arguably lesser known and certainly underutilized in a program like Illustrator.

Unlike a Pathfinder crop or trim command, a clipping path (created using the Clipping Mask command in the dropdown menu) remains live and editable at all times. The art that has been cropped still exists outside the boundary of the clipping path and can be edited, repositioned in the mask, or released from the mask at any time. Opacity masks are created by using the luminosity of one object to change the visibility of another.

Clipping paths and opacity masks can be any shape or size and can be combined.

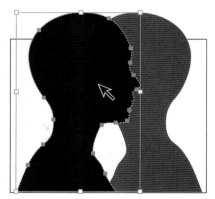

Making a clipping path.
A basic clipping path consists of two pieces of art, painted in any way. The object to be used as the mask must be on top. In this example, the black silhouette will mask the underlying red silhouette. Choose both object and select Object > Clipping Mask > Make from the menu.

The clipping path applied.
The clipping path loses its fill and stroke once it is applied. The object now behaves as though it is a single object (similar to being grouped). To eliminate the mask effect, choose Object > Clipping Mask > Release.

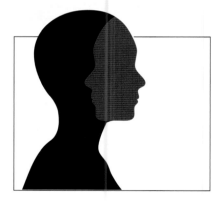

Fill clipping path with color.
To fill the mask with color, direct-select the path and click on a color swatch. The process would be the same as adding a stroke to the path.

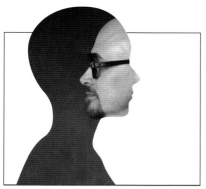

Clipping path with placed bitmap image.
Clipping paths can be used with placed, linked bitmaps.

Multiple clipping paths with placed bitmap image.
A series of clipping paths can be used to mask different areas of a single placed bitmap. Select only the clipping paths and create a compound path. Make sure the path is on top of the bitmap and choose the Make Clipping command.

Clipping an existing clipping path.
The final image from the top right was duplicated and clipped again using the text outlines "FACE." The face inside the letters has been modified using a transparency effect and the letters have had a drop shadow applied.

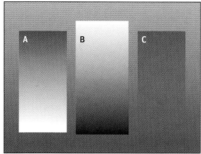

Basic opacity masks.
Vector gradients have one significant limitation: they don't allow for transparency. Opacity masks overcome this limitation. A is a simple gradient; B is a grayscale gradient drawn on top of A; and C is the result of the opacity mask. The gradient now blends seamlessly into the background.

Combining clipping paths and opacity masks.
Multiple clipping paths and opacity masks can be combined. The user must be vigilant relative to the size and complexity of the file to ensure that it will print. There is no hard and fast rule for this. Trial and error is the best teacher.

Increasing complexity.
A bitmap pattern has been traced for the background and a three-tone opacity mask applied. The head and face clipping group now includes a portion of the background pattern and a transparency effect applied to it. This is still a relatively small file, maintains all of the benefits of drawing with vectors, and will print successfully.

Simple gradients and transparency modes.
Created using only basic gradients and various transparency effects, this is a typical use of vectors to create an illustration.

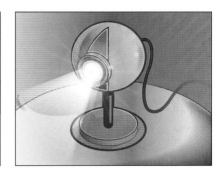

Adding opacity masks.
The same illustration utilizing the gradients and transparency settings as well as adding in details using opacity masks. The opportunity with these masks is to create art that can have softer edges and a more organic feel while maintaining the benefits of vectors.

Synthesis

Transparency and blending may be among the most valuable assets to be found in vector applications (and indeed, in most bitmap programs as well). When used in conjunction with other features, transparency creates an almost infinite variety of illustrative possibilities.

Transparency and Blending Modes, which can be considered as a single feature, were introduced into vector applications relatively recently in digital time. It was a quantum leap in the opportunities it afforded the designer. Any vector program without it would not be able to compete in the market. It is an absolute must in Adobe Illustrator, Adobe Flash, Adobe After Effects, and in many other types of applications.

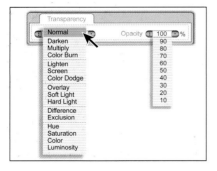

Transparency and Blending Mode palette.
The palette offers two dropdown menus: one to control the blending mode of an object (its effect on colors underneath), and one the transparency (the value of a color). These two properties can, and often are, applied to the same selected object.

Blending Modes.
The nature of each blending mode is complex and somewhat perplexing in definition. The only practical way to see the effects is to create a grid (similar to that above). The result of the application of a Blending mode is entirely dependent on the properties of any object(s) underneath.

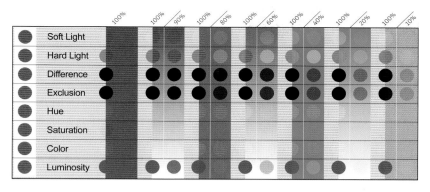

	100%	100%	90%	100%	80%	100%	60%	100%	40%	100%	20%	100%	10%
Soft Light													
Hard Light													
Difference													
Exclusion													
Hue													
Saturation													
Color													
Luminosity													

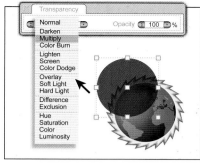

Transparency

Normal — Opacity 100 %

Normal
Darken
Multiply
Color Burn
Lighten
Screen
Color Dodge
Overlay
Soft Light
Hard Light
Difference
Exclusion
Hue
Saturation
Color
Luminosity

Blending Modes and Transparency.
A demonstration of the combination of transparency and blending modes. The change of value can have dramatic effects on the results achieved. Layering objects of different colors, transparency, and blending can offer the designer a wide range of creative opportunities.

Applying a Blending Mode or Transparency.
Select an object or group and click and hold on the mode dropdown or the opacity dropdown and select the desired property. Any object or group can have both a transparency and a blend applied.

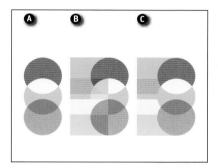

Blending Modes, Transparency, and stacking.
In A, objects of different colors, Blending Modes, and values have been stacked. In B, squares are introduced beneath every other circle. In C, the circles have been grouped (forcing them to the front). With the circles selected, choose Show Options > Isolate Blending in the palette options. This isolates the two sets of objects, maintaining the blending modes.

The Isolate Blending feature.
At far left, all elements are 100% and "normal" blending. In the center, the "S" and its outline are set to "hard light." At the far right, the outline is set to "hard light" and the "S" is set to "lighten."

Blending Modes, Transparency, and placed objects.
Placed bitmaps, linked or embedded, can have any mode, transparency, or combination of both applied. (Blending Modes Normal and Transparency 100%).

Various Transparency values and Blending Modes.
Apple: Multiply 100%
Type: Screen 50%
Circle: Normal 100%

Apple: Hard light 100%
Type: Overlay 65%
Circle: Color Burn 100%

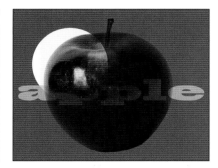

Apple: Brought to top of object stack, feathered Multiply 95%
Type: Normal 100%
Circle: Normal 100%

Tutorial:
Sequential Pattern Recognition

Patterns, symbols, appearances, and styles make use of the most fundamental and unique aspect of vectors: the definition and description of objects using mathematical statements.

Vector graphics can be thought of as modular objects. This characteristic provides a significant advantage over bitmaps. Because they are snippets of text (the mathematical descriptions) they can be used in situations that require patterns, styles, or art objects that require multiple uses in situations other than patterns. These modular objects are called instances: references to objects rather than the objects themselves. This requires less memory and creates smaller files. It is also an important feature of 3D programs.

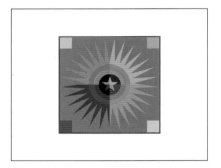

Create art for geometric pattern.
Creating art to use as a pattern employs the drawing techniques you have already acquired, with certain limitations.* After the art is created, draw a box around the art that is unfilled and unstroked. This box represents the boundary of the tile. The red box here is for clarity only.

Fill shape with a pattern.
With the tile selected, choose Edit > Define Pattern. This will place the pattern in the swatches palette. Draw a shape and click on the pattern icon in the swatches palette (as a fill). This will fill the shape with the repeating pattern.

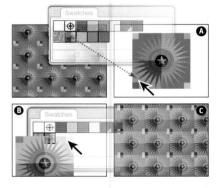

Global changes to a pattern.
Drag the original pattern tile from the swatches palette to the artboard (A). Edit the art, Option/Alt drag, and release the new art over the previous tile icon (B). All instances of that "master object" will change because they reference the original art (C).

Create art for organic seamless pattern.
Similar to building a geometric pattern, an organic pattern requires that all four sides meet and create a seamless pattern (the crop marks aid in constructing the tile). Fill the center of the tile with random elements and release the crop marks to create the tile boundary.

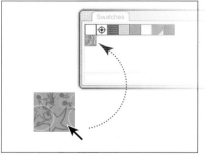

Drag tile art to Swatches palette.
Another method for defining a pattern tile is to simply drag it into the swatches palette.

Draw shape and apply pattern fill.
Filling the shape with the pattern is the same as for the figure top right. It is not necessary for the filled shape to be rectangular. In addition, effects and transformations can be applied to the shape and the pattern.

*Patterns, gradients, blends, meshes, bitmaps, graphs, or masks can't be used in a pattern tile.

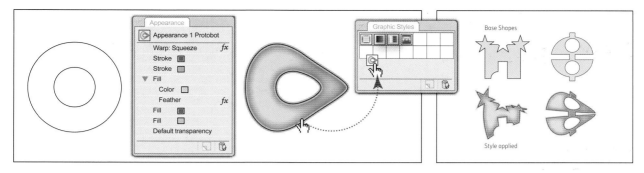

Creating appearance attributes.

Appearances are a collection of attributes that can be saved as a graphic style (similar to text styles in page layout programs). These graphic styles can be applied, edited, or removed at any time without changing the underlying object (such as the doughnut shape above).

Saving an appearance as a graphic style.

After an object is edited using the Appearance palette, the object is dragged into the Graphic Styles palette. All of the appearance attributes are stored in a style. This simply allows the user to name, access, and apply the appearance conveniently.

Applying an appearance.

Applying a graphic style is consistent with applying any other attribute to an object. Click on the desired graphic, then click on the appropriate style in the palette. This applies the style to the original shapes.

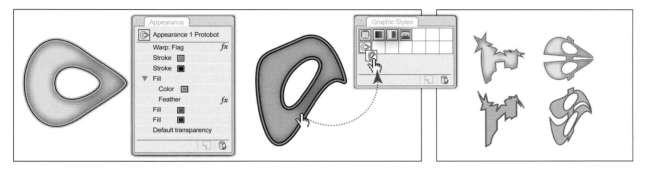

Editing an appearance.

A graphic style is chosen, revealing its properties in the Appearance palette. These properties can be modified at will. The graphic style and all instances will update. Alternately, a graphic style is dragged to the artboard, edited, and added to the Style palette. This preserves the original style and creates a new one. The new style can be applied using the standard method. The edited style can also be Option/Alt dragged over the initial graphic style to replace it. This change will be reflected in objects that had the original style applied to them. The top tier of this figure contains the original style applied to the shapes. The bottom tier illustrates the result of editing the appearance and style.

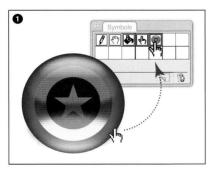
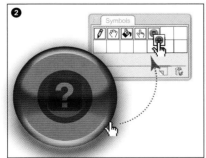

Creating and using Symbols.

Symbols are another powerful use of instances to create more complex graphics and maintain relatively small file sizes. A symbol can be made from almost any piece of art by dragging it into the Symbols palette (1). It can be edited by changing the original art and replacing the symbol in the Symbols palette (2: Option/Alt drag over the original symbol). Symbols have very specific advantages, many too complex to include here. The essence of a symbol is its efficiency and flexibility. A symbol can be transformed and altered like any other object—immediately changing the instances in a design where a symbol has been used over and over. Symbols also have special tools associated with them. Figure 3 is the result of the "symbol sprayer." This tool works something like an airbrush, spraying symbols instead. Figure 4 is the result of replacing the original symbol with a revision (2). This replaces the instances in 3 with the revised symbol from 2.

Tutorial:
Alphabot

At this point, the most critical aspects of the use of a vector-drawing application have been covered. To a large extent, this information has focused on color and permutations of the use of color. If the basics have been mastered, these tools add the sheen and luster that can set one execution apart from another.

What can't be overlooked here is the necessity for strong skills in color and color theory. Color is so easily accessible that there can be a tendency to start randomly applying colors. This can lead to a less successful result and waste precious time. Before beginning to color the art, work out a strong palette by experimenting with different color approaches. Once you have that palette (sometimes referred to as a "colorway"), executing the final art becomes more efficient and more satisfying. In the end, it exhibits the cohesiveness found in excellent illustration or other final uses.

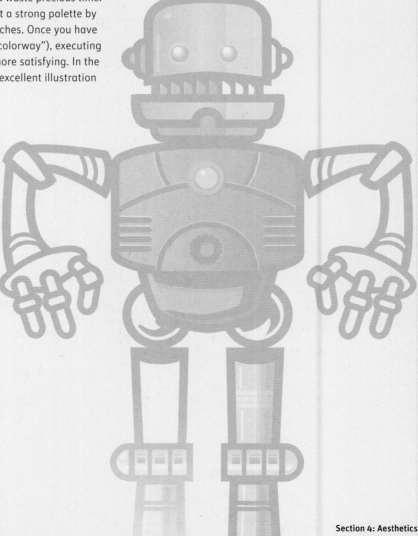

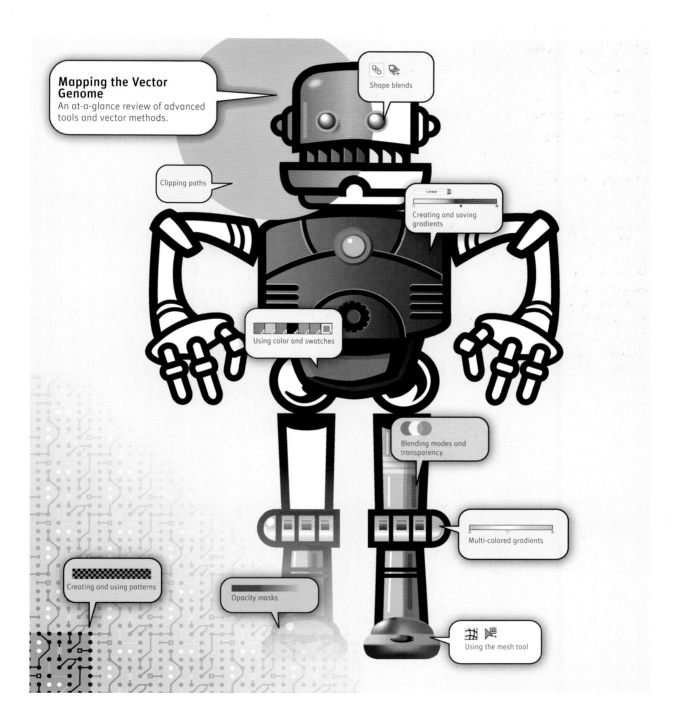

Artist profile:
Catalina Estrada

Country of origin: Colombia
(now living in Spain)

Primary software: Adobe® Illustrator®

Primary fields: Advertising, editorial,
fashion, product/package illustration,
fine art

URL: catalinaestrada.com

Born in Medellin, Colombia, Catalina Estrada graduated
with a degree in graphic design from the University Pontificia
Bolivariana (Medellin). In 1999, she moved to Barcelona,
Spain, where she studied fine arts at the Llotja School of Arts,
where she specialized in lithography. She started working in
vectors in 2001, and the controlled complexity of her artwork
has won her many clients, including Coca-Cola, Sony Music,
Nike, and fashion brands Anunciação and Paul Smith.

1

2

"My mother's love of color has been a great influence on my work," Estrada says. "I'm influenced by many Latin American artists, writers, and musicians, and I am inspired by almost anything that touches my emotions."

After moving to Barcelona, Estrada realized how much she missed the contact with nature she had enjoyed as a child in the Colombian countryside. "But at the same time," she adds, "being able to be in touch with lots of different cultures in this city has been amazing for my work. I have also been very lucky to have traveled a lot, and this has been a great influence in all I do."

When it comes to commercial illustration clients, Estrada says there's always little time to develop the projects, so she starts sketching in the computer right away. "I work in Adobe Illustrator on a Wacom tablet—that's it," she says.

For her personal projects, Estrada often sketches on paper before moving into Adobe Illustrator. "I work on the color palette and the composition at the same time," she explains. "I'm a bit obsessed with color and details, so I can spend lots of time when it comes to the final color combination."

3

4

1. Illustrated limited-edition bottle for Coca-Cola, released in Australia for an Easter campaign.
2. Illustration for Brazilian fashion brand Anunciação's spring/ summer 2008 collection.
3. CD cover for Taiwanese singer Chow Huei (Sony Music).
4. Illustrations for *Nike Air* art magazine.

All images © 2007 Catalina Estrada.

Artist profile:
Nancy Stahl

Country of origin: USA

Primary software: Adobe® Illustrator®, Corel® Painter™, Adobe® Photoshop®

Primary fields: Wide range of media

URLs: nancystahl.com, illoz.com/stahl

With her elegant use of color and her imaginative use of vector techniques, Nancy Stahl has become one of the world's most high-profile vector artists. She studied illustration at Art Center College of Design before moving to New York City to begin her freelance career.

Her work has been reproduced as large as billboards for the Goodwill Games and the city of Memphis, Tennessee, and as small as postage stamps for the US Postal Service. She has created packaging and identity illustrations for companies including Time-Life Records, Scharffen Berger Cocoa, and Stonyfield Farms. She also worked as artistic director on a television commercial for M&Ms. Recent print work of hers has appeared in *The New York Times*, *Der Spiegel* magazine, *The New Republic*, on calendars for Workman Publishing, and in publications for Sappi Papers.

1

2

Stahl was chairman of the Society of Illustrators Annual in 2000 and has taught illustration at the School of Visual Arts, the Fashion Institute of Technology, Syracuse University Independent Study Degree Program, and the MFA program at the University of Hartford.

While Stahl prefers to paint in Corel Painter, she says most of her clients prefer her more identifiable vector style: "flat-graphic, poster-like, and slightly retro." This style has evolved to include adding a dot screen and some "airbrushing" in Adobe Photoshop. Her interests also extend to textiles and crafts, and her portfolio includes a section of knitted and embroidered images used as illustration. "I draw in Adobe Illustrator, then import to my embroidery program, download via a card to my sewing machine, then it stitches out the designs," says Stahl.

92

According to artist and critic Charley Parker, "Stahl's boldly graphic images, whether painterly or rendered in vectors, have a terrific sense of color and design, and are textbook examples of how to see and isolate the geometric forms produced by volume, light, and shadow. Hidden planes reveal themselves, and people, objects, and landscapes shift between representational images and pure design."

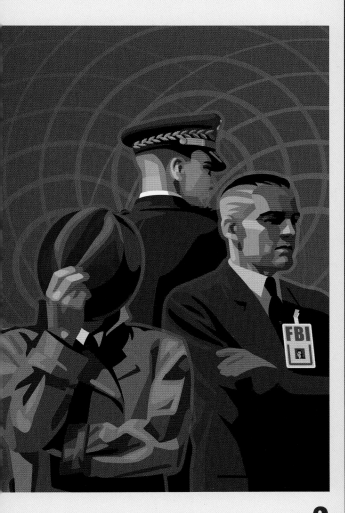

3

4

1. Self-promotional piece (Workbook) redrawn in Adobe Illustrator from an original gouache painting for the fashion section of German *Esquire* magazine.
2. Illustration for Amdahl Annual Report.
3. Cover image for *Security Management*.
4. Series of trade ads for Torani Syrup. Client: Amazon Advertising.

   All images © 2007 Nancy Stahl.

Artist profile:
Cristiano Siqueira (aka CrisVector)

Country of origin: Brazil

Primary fields: Editorial, advertising

Primary software: Adobe® Illustrator®, Poser®

URLs: crisvector.deviantart.com, crisvector.com

Cristiano Siqueira is an illustrator from São Paulo, Brazil, whose work encompasses a wide range of print illustrations, CD and book covers, and toy packaging designs, among other projects. His work is notable for its beautiful drawing and rendering, vibrant color, and sophisticated use of shape blends.

"The Brazilian culture influences me with its colors, mood, beautiful women, and the power of the simple people," says Siqueira, "although I can't call myself a 'genuine' Brazilian artist because I still need to dive more deeply into my cultural roots and produce art free from the influences of other cultures." Foremost among those influences are Francis Bacon, Pablo Picasso, Japanese illustrator Ippei Gyoubu, Brazilian

1. Queen of Hearts: Illustration produced on Adobe Illustrator 10 and Poser 6 for DepthCore International Digital Art Group.

2 & 6. Harlequin: Self-promotional illustration produced using Adobe Illustrator 10 and Poser 6.

3. Timbaland: Illustration for an article about the music producer Timbaland, his album *Shock Value*, and his marketing strategy (Abril Publishing/ *Bizz Magazine*).

4. Colombina: Self-promotional portrait of the artist's wife from over a photo taken by cell phone.

5. Mohawk: Self-promotional vector illustration done over an Adobe Photoshop sketch drawn by tablet. First work of a miniseries of pinup girls posted at DeviantArt.com. Received the "Daily Deviation" feature given by the site's directors.

All images © 2007 Cristiano Siqueira.

1

2

94

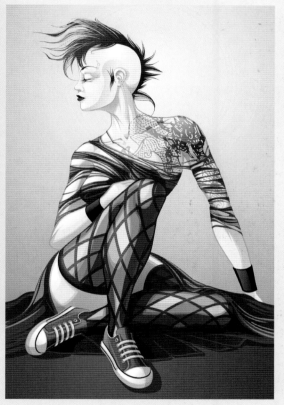

illustrator Kako, and American comics artist Bill Sienkiewicz. Siqueira has attracted attention for his excellent digital portraits, which combine the use of vector and 3D applications. "I'm trying to represent and distort reality, always striving to be quicker, more detailed, and more precise," he says. In creating such images, he usually starts by sketching on paper to clarify ideas or study the best composition for the scene. "It's largely an intuitive process," he comments. After the concept is defined, Siqueira gathers references—sometimes scanned photos and sometimes 3D models created using e frontier's Poser software, with which he is able to experiment with poses and lighting. The work is then refined and completed in Adobe Illustrator 10.

Artist Profile: Cristiano Siqueira (aka CrisVector)

Text Support

Support

5

Tutorial:
Type Casting

Typography is one of the most, if not the most, important aspects of a designer's responsibility. Words and pictures integrate into a whole, communicating ideas and evoking emotions. Most design is not as effective if one of the two is absent.

The copy (content) provided by a copywriter, author, or editor is the meat of the design process. The conventional wisdom is that graphic design, advertising, television, and most of the communication media we see are becoming more "image" oriented, that is, less reliant on words. The everyday design, though, still focuses on the clarity and expressiveness of typography to support and augment the meaning of words. Design, especially type usage, is in service to the word. That being said, options for unique, often outrageous, creative use of type is a hallmark of vector art.

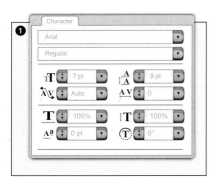

The Character palette.
The character palette offers control over every aspect of the basic characteristics of a setting of type. Style, size, leading (the very basics) start here.

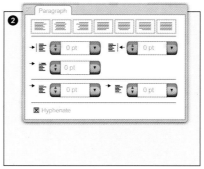

The Paragraph palette.
The essentials for control over type alignment (center, flush left) indents and hyphenation are set here.

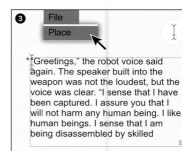

Importing (placing) text.
After drawing a rectangle, click in it with the text tool (inset), and choose File > Place. This will present a directory dialog to select a text file to be imported into the box. Select a file and click on Place. The text will import and fill the rectangle. The red box in the lower right of the text block indicates "overflow" (text that doesn't fit in the box).

* Excerpt from I, Robot © 2005, Cory Doctorow.

98

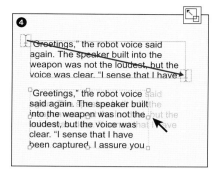

4

Importing text while drawing a bounding box.
Here, an alternative to 3 was used to create a text box. Draw a bounding box with the text tool by clicking and dragging the text tool from the upper left to lower right, approximating the desired size and placement. This places the text directly. The bounding box can be resized and the text reflows with it (bottom example).

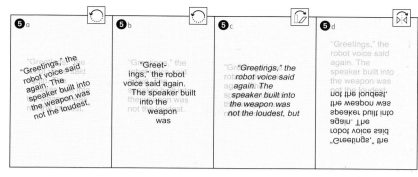

5a **5**b **5**c **5**d

Transformation of text in a bounding box.
Rotating text in a bounding box requires different considerations from text entered at a point (as in 8). In 5a, the text box was selected by clicking inside the box and rotating. In 5b, only the bounding box was selected. The effect on the text is obvious and generally undesirable. Other transforms (skew and reflect shown here) perform as expected.

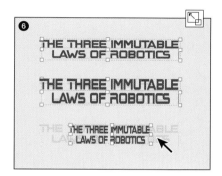

6

Text entered at a point.
Adjusting the bounding box of text entered at a point (directly onto the artboard) distorts type in undesirable ways, often decreasing readability.

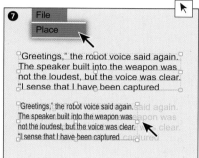

7

Text placed without a text or bounding box.
In addition, body text placed without a text box cannot be reflowed or re-ragged. Manipulating the bounding box (above, bottom example) simply squeezes or stretches the text similarly to 6.

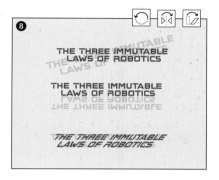

8

Transformation of text entered at a point.
Text entered directly to the artboard (see 6) can be transformed exactly like any other object. The examples here demonstrate the effects of common transformations.

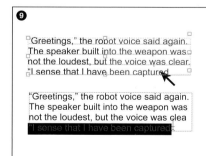

9

Selecting text.
There are two basic methods for selecting text. First, clicking on the bounding box with the pointer. In this scenario changes affect everything in the bounding box (top, red was chosen from the Swatch palette). The second option is to use the type tool to drag-select specific text (bottom), and change the attributes of the text. This method also allows changes to specific areas without affecting others.

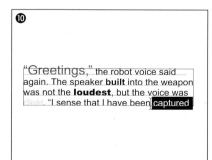

10

Selections and applying different styles.
Using the text tool to make specific selections allows for the application of different styles. As many styles as desired can be used. While not particularly valuable in paragraph text, it can be used imaginatively in display text.

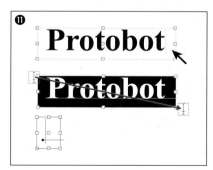

11

Deleting text and empty type paths.
Deleting text is straightforward, with one caveat. By selecting and deleting the bounding box, the text is removed completely. Deleting just the text will leave an empty (invisible) bounding box. This can cause problems later.

New Word Order

Word processing in a vector program has developed over the years. In the early stages of development, only very basic text editing was available. The demand to create finished, ready-to-print documents demanded more robust word processing features.

Previously, in "Type Casting," clear concepts and the mechanics of typography were introduced, including the transformation and manipulation of text as a graphic. Word processing is specifically concerned with the entry and editing of running text (as in text found in a book or manual) and some of the nuances associated with the setting of type. There are some very small and often overlooked details that demonstrate the difference between professional typesetting and obvious amateur or novice attempts.

"G reetings," the robot voice said again. The speaker built into the weapon was not the loudest, but the voice was clear. "I sense that I have been captured. I assure you that I will not harm any

Basic word processing.
The process of entering text into a vector document is, not surprisingly, very much like word processing in almost any other graphics program. A text box is drawn using the text tool or the rectangle primitive and text is entered directly, pasted, or placed into the text box.

"G reetings," the robot voice said again. The speaker built into the weapon was not the loudest, but the voice was clear. "I sense that I have been captured. I assure you that I will not harm any human being. I

Smart punctuation.
Generally not a problem in dedicated word processing and layout applications, graphics applications are still not as sophisticated in some typographic nuances. An important example is open and closed quotation marks and apostrophes. By default, the feet and inches (previous figure inset) marks are used. Text must be selected and the smart punctuation attribute applied. This difference will often differentiate the novice from the professional.

¶Greetings,"·the·robot·voice· said·again.·The·speaker· built·into·the·weapon·was·n ot·the·loudest,·but·the· voice·was·clear.·"I·sense· that·I·have·been·captured.·I assure·you·that·I·will·not· harm·any·human·being.·I·lik

Show hidden characters.
Hidden characters include spaces, tabs and paragraph returns. Eliminating extra spaces, adding missing spaces, or troubleshooting text that doesn't seem to behave in expected ways are common uses of the "show hidden characters" command. One of the most important uses is the elimination of the extra space at the end of a sentence. Text imported from other word processing programs will often include two spaces at the end of a paragraph. The extra space is not used in professional typesetting.

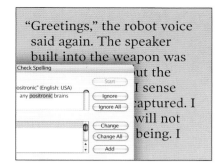

Check spelling.
An indispensable feature of word processing is spell checking. Added in the last few years to vector applications, it is crucial in a complete set of word processing tools. The spell checker flags words in the document, allowing the user to substitute a suggested correction or to ignore it and move on.

Adding a word to the dictionary.
During the spell checking process, an opportunity is provided to add words to the program's dictionary that are uncommon, trade specific, or imaginary. This speeds up the spell checking on subsequent documents.

Find and replace.
The Find and Replace function provides an efficient way of changing characters that appear frequently and need to be edited. This includes text styles as well as letters and words.

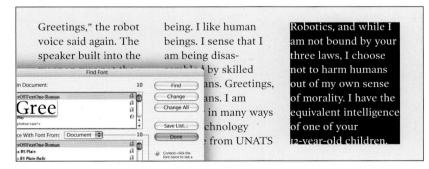

Linked columns.
Columns can be linked as demonstrated previously. The process is different than in a layout program, but the result is the same. Linked text boxes allow overflow text to run into another text box. Text boxes can be linked and unlinked at will.

Hyphenation.
Basic hyphenation options are accessed through the paragraph palette, including turning hyphenation on and off and accessing the advanced features (the blue insets). The upper blue inset highlights the flyout menu access arrow. This invokes the Hyphenation dialog to set more advanced hyphenation settings, which are particularly important in justified text.

Find Font.
Similar in concept to Find and Replace, Find Font provides a relatively painless method for finding every instance of a font in a document (particularly a missing font) and replacing it with a different font on a global basis.

Export text.
While we generally don't use a vector program as the primary tool for word processing, there are times when text has been composed directly in the vector application or extensive editing has occurred in place. This might precipitate the need to export text to allow it to be edited by another team member.

Programming Language

The type specification establishes the way type is set. Knowledge of fonts, style, leading, and kerning, and a grasp of how these variables can be controlled, are imperative for solid design solutions and necessary before taking advantage of some of the more interesting type tools.

Before the advent of the "desktop publishing" revolution and the evolution of the tools related to typography, specifying type was a mysterious, arcane process that required no small degree of experience. Even though the process of setting type today appears "easy," it still requires an understanding of readability, legibility, and color. While this is not the forum to define all of the more advanced concepts in setting type, awareness of these issues is vital. Here we explore the basic mechanics and techniques for setting type.

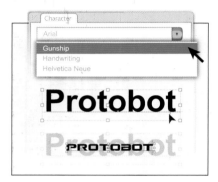

Choosing fonts.
Fonts can be chosen from the Type menu or, as shown in this example, from the Character palette. All previous specs remain (size, leading, color) when a font style is changed.

Basic type specifications.
Still in the Character palette, the size of the text can be chosen in the size dropdown menu. Text must be selected individually to change discrete words in a setting. Points are the traditional unit of measure for type.

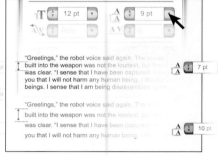

Leading.
The Character palette also presents the user with leading options. Leading is the distance from the baseline of one line to the baseline of another. With the text or the bounding box selected, choose the desired leading or enter it manually in the box next to the dropdown menu.

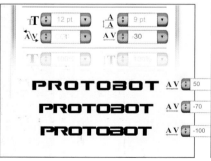

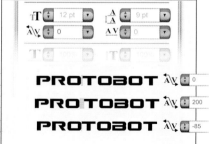

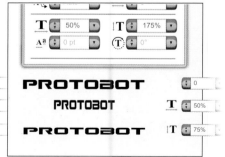

Tracking.
Tracking controls the spacing of the text, keeping the same amount throughout the selection based on the type designer's original optimized letter and word spacing. This can be useful in small increments. The greater the tracking, the more certain aberrations become apparent.

Kerning.
Kerning refers to the space between two letters. Ts and Ys can offer some problematic letter spacing. With the text tool inserted between the letters, you can increase or decrease the space between them without affecting any other type. Kerning is often more important in large type where letter-spacing problems become more apparent.

Horizontal and vertical scale.
Horizontal and vertical scale options can create artificially condensed or expanded type. While this is common practice, it is undesirable. It severely damages the characteristics of the type design and is a sign of a lack of appreciation for the subtleties of font design.

 102

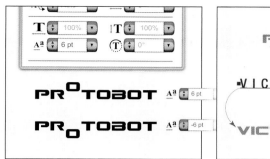

Baseline shift.
The baseline raises or lowers the selected type a specific distance above or below the current baseline. This can be used as an alternative to a superscript or subscript and is useful when setting text along a path (covered later).

Copying text attributes.
The eyedropper is used to apply the text attributes of one setting of type to another. The type to be changed is selected (center), the eyedropper is clicked on text with the desired styles (top), and those attributes are then applied to the selected text (bottom).

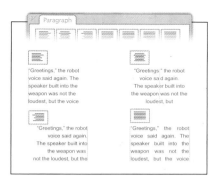

Text alignment.
The paragraph palette offers the choice of various text alignment operations. Illustrated above: flush left, centered, flush right, and justified.

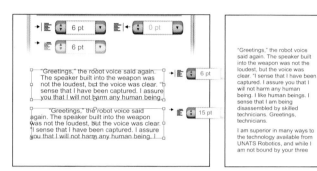

Indentation.
The Paragraph palette also offers options for indenting text. Entire selections of text can be indented left (top) and right or the first line in running text to create paragraph breaks.

Spaces before and after paragraphs.
Another common method for creating breaks between paragraphs in running text is to specify the distance between paragraphs (referred to as secondary leading in traditional typesetting). This is often used in place of indents to create paragraph breaks.

Hyphenation and Justification.
Hyphenation and Justification is a more complex set of options that affect the type, along with tracking and kerning that may have already been applied. Applying hyphenation is fairly simple with ragged type. Justification only controls the spacing of type that has been set to align both left and right. Hyphenation and justification are used together when setting justified type in an effort to create natural word and letter spacing.

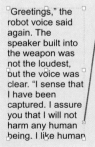

Threaded text.
Threaded text flows through multiple bounding boxes, similar to a page-layout application. To create threaded text, draw at least two rectangles and select them. Choose Type > Threaded Text > Create. This will create linked boxes. Placed text will flow into both text boxes.

Setting type in an irregular shape.
Body text has some commonly used techniques that also involve paths. Text can be set in a shape of any kind. Doing this well will take some patience and experimentation.

Setting type with a runaround.
Type that runs around another object (this includes any object, including other text) can be set by placing an object in the desired position, selecting both the text and the object and choosing menu item Object > Text Wrap > Make. This is a common technique to add interest to long passages of running text.

Face Facts

Display faces are those designed to be used exclusively at large sizes, although many contemporary font families include distinct styles for both display and text sizes. Originally developed for advertising use, and often elaborate and decorative, they are intended to catch readers' attention. With readability a secondary consideration, display fonts should not be used for longer passages of text.

Display faces run the gamut from traditional fonts expertly retooled for use at large sizes to those that might be called gimmicky, or for what seems to be relatively little practical use. From the illustrative typography of Victorian broadsides to the avalanche of unusual typefaces created with current font software, display faces can be visually compelling and offer the potential to evoke just the right emotional response from the reader. Fonts designed for use as display faces can also be good starting points for logotype design.

HELLO WORLD

Hello World

Hello world.
The face on top is ITC Anna, designed by Daniel Pelavin. Underneath is Times Roman, probably one of the most ubiquitous fonts, used primarily as a text face because of its readability at smaller sizes and narrow column widths. It was included as one of the original sets of fonts on the Apple Macintosh when it was introduced in 1984.

"GREETINGS," THE ROBOT VOICE SAID AGAIN. THE SPEAKER BUILT INTO THE WEAPON WAS NOT THE LOUDEST, BUT THE VOICE WAS CLEAR. "I SENSE THAT I HAVE BEEN CAPTURED. I ASSURE YOU THAT I WILL NOT HARM ANY HUMAN BEING. I LIKE HUMAN BEINGS. I SENSE THAT I AM BEING DISASSEMBLED BY SKILLED

A display face in a paragraph setting.
ITC Anna is a beautiful, art deco–inspired typeface that can lend a sense of casual elegance to a design. Unfortunately it does not, and definitely was not designed to, work well in a text setting.

"Greetings," the robot voice said again. The speaker built into the weapon was not the loudest, but the voice was clear. "I sense that I have been captured. I assure you that I will not harm any human being. I

Text font in text setting.
Immediately evident, especially because of its proximity to the previous example, this is clearly a font intended for longer settings of text.

104

i, robot

by Cory Doctorow

"Greetings," the robot voice said again. The speaker built into the weapon was not the loudest, but the voice was clear. "I sense that I have been captured. I assure you that I will not harm any human being. I like human beings. I sense that I am being disassembled by skilled technicians. Greetings, technicians. I am superior

in many ways to the technology available from UNATS Robotics, and while I am not bound by your three laws, I choose not to harm humans out of my own sense of morality. I have the equivalent intelligence of one of your 12-year-old children. In Eurasia, many positronic brain

Headlines, pull quotes, and decks.
The typeface used here for the headline and pull quote is called "Fung Foo." The playful quality of the type and its unusual shapes makes it an extremely poor candidate for running text. At headline and pull-quote size, however, it suggests eastern iconography, calligraphy, and the machine age—a look that seems oddly fitting for this imaginative tale of Asimovian robots. The headline demonstrates the need, especially important here, for kerning type at this size. The gray type behind the headline is the default kerning before adjustments were made.

Logotypes.
Display fonts can also provide a valuable base for logo or other illustrative typographic use. Top: the headline with a simple graphic change. Bottom: Helvetica (a typeface often criticized for overuse) is transformed by a series of simple changes.

Other decorative effects.
Although not limited to display faces, various outline treatments can be used to add dimension or other graphic interest. The flexibility of outlines and strokes in vector applications makes these experiments fast and productive.

Trying on different faces.
Display faces, all type really, can reach a point where type becomes image. In these examples, various display faces have been modified using common vector tools. Figure 1 uses various inline effects (where strokes and lines are used inside of the letterform) to create interesting graphic choices. In 2, offset outlines are used to similar effect.

Display text as masks.
Last, but definitely not least, interesting display faces can make masks for art or photography. Sometimes this can be a way to "help" a bad photograph or to add texture or other art that transforms the text even further.

Machine Language

After the basic, professional use of typography is mastered, the real fun starts. In a vector program, type can be bent, twisted, stretched, and otherwise teased into creative contortions. Make your type twist and shout.

The tools for these transformations are varied, with multiple methods of implementation. They are often used in series to achieve a specific look for an object. A virtually unlimited range of transformations is possible. The basics are presented here with the caveat that, after learning the basic uses of each tool, it is necessary to explore them to appreciate fully the creative opportunities they represent.

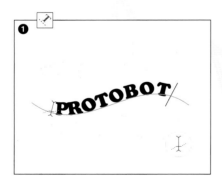

Type on a path.
Setting type on a path requires a path, open or closed, and the type on a path tool. As the tool approaches the line it will change to the symbol shown in the inset. The type is limited only by the length of the path.

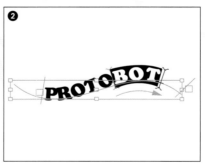

Editing text on a path.
Text on a path can be selected in the same way as any other text and can be kerned, tracked, or changed using any of the type specification options. Text on a path will almost always require kerning.

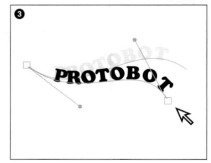

Editing the path.
Selecting an anchor point with the direct-selection tool and dragging the point or the direction handles will change the nature of the path. The text will flow along the path as it is manipulated.

④

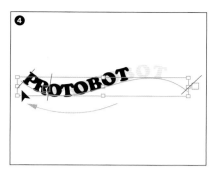

Changing position of text on a path.
There are three control lines associated with the text: the left, the center, and the right (shown in red). Clicking on these control handles allows for movement of the text along the path by dragging the line.

⑤

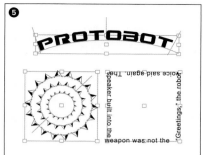

Various paths with type.
Type can be aligned with any path. They can be open paths like the top example or closed shapes like the circle and square in 5. On the left is a series of concentric circles that have a dingbat applied to the paths. This can work very well for a decorative effect. Bottom right is type on the path of a rectangle. This is harder to control because the type must turn corners, but the possibility is there. Figure 6 illustrates type on a spiral. As a general rule, type on a path works best on objects without sharp corners.

⑥

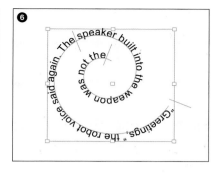

⑦

Changing orientation of type on a path.
Using the same control handles as in 4, dragging the center up or down will change the orientation of the text on the path (inside or outside the arc).

⑧

Setting vertical type.
Different tools are available for setting type in a vertical configuration. The icon representing each option is illustrated at top from left to right: type set on a straight vertical, type set on a curved path, type set on a vertical with the common orientation (left to right), and the same setting rotated.

⑨

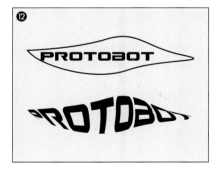

Warp: Arc

Warp: Bulge

Warp: Flag

Warp effects.
Warp effects are a common function in vector applicaions with advanced type capabilites. For all intents and purposes, warp effects are readymade paths and envelopes that allow for easy interactive editing of your text. Multiple effects can be applied to the same text, layering a series of modifications.

⑩

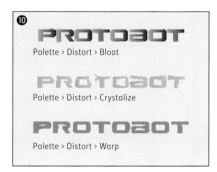

Palette > Distort > Bloat

Palette > Distort > Crystalize

Palette > Distort > Warp

Distortion tools in the Tool palette.
There are several methods for accessing different type and graphic effects. The tool palette offers different tools that provide distortion. The same tools are found in the menu, except the warp tool in the palette, which is for more organic changes. As shown in 9, the warp tools in the menu provide a very different set of options. The options in the tool palette can be difficult to control. The default settings are far too dramatic. These effects also increase the file size considerably.

⑪

Effect Menu > Scribble

Effect Menu > Stylize > Round Corners
Effect Menu > Stylize > Rough Pastels

Effect Menu > Pixelate > Color Halftone

Photoshop effects.
Many of the filters available in Adobe Photoshop can be applied in Adobe Illustrator. These changes are nondestructive, leaving the text editable, and the effects can be changed or removed. To make an effect permanent, choose Object > Expand Appearance. The object is converted to an embedded bitmap.

⑫

Envelope distortion.
Envelope distortions are interesting options for manipulating type and objects. While the process can become much more complex than this (with meshes and added warps), this demonstrates the basic use. A closed path is drawn around the object you want to distort. Select the object and the path (the path should be the frontmost object) and choose the menu item Object > Object Distort > Make with Top Object. The object and the path remain editable.

Identification Specification

After a rough design for the ProtoBot Logo, the basic typographic tools that have been covered have been brought to bear on its execution.

The creation of artwork similar to this should make judicious use of layers. While not specifically covered here, layers for each of the components will speed up the process by allowing easy isolation of each component.

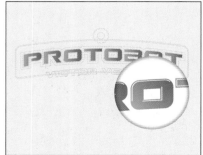

Type on a path with a warp applied.
Warp tools and the text on a path are used to build the basic type. A gradient is created and is used to fill the type.

Creating a highlight.
The outside paths of the font are offset inward (a negative offset) and parts of the paths are deleted to create an inline highlight.

Background outline effect.
The original type is copied and hidden. After pasting the copied logo in back (this puts it directly behind the hidden logo) the text is filled again.

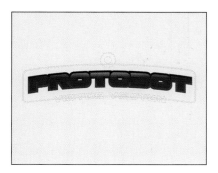

Editing the background type.
The type has now had a gradient stroked outline applied.

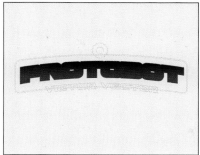

Adding a modified layer behind the type.
The text is copied, hidden, and pasted in back. The outline is stroked with a heavier weight, converted to outlines, and, using Pathfinder, merged into one shape.

The addition of a warped rectangle.
A rectangle is drawn around the type. The same warp from the first step is applied. All filters are still "live" at this point.

Further decorative effects applied to rectangle.
Using the offset command again, the curved box is offset and gray is applied. That shape is offset again and the dark background color is applied.

Descriptor type set and the same warp applied.
Using the same typeface and the same warp, the secondary type is set. At this point all of the changes have been non-destructive.

Expand the logo.
The secondary type is outlined with the background color and the object is expanded, committing to all of the changes and making the effects permanent.

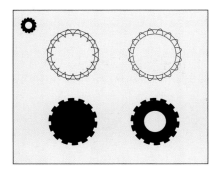

Creating the gear.
The gear is created by dragging a star primitive and increasing the number of points on the star. A shape is created to trim the tops of the points to create the basic gear. The inner opening, to finish the gear, is a compound path.

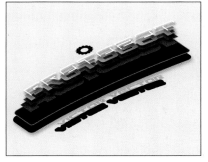

An exploded view of the logo.
This exploded view provides a view of the various steps used to create the logo, and clarifies the stacking order.

Expanded and grouped, the final logo.

Artist profile:
Rian Hughes

Country of origin: UK

Primary software: Adobe® Illustrator®, Fontographer

Primary fields: Wide range of media

URL: devicefonts.co.uk

Rian Hughes studied at the London College of Printing and, under the name Device, provides design, custom type, and illustration for advertising campaigns, record sleeves, book jackets, graphic novels, and television. He has contributed to numerous international exhibitions and lectured internationally.

A one-man show of Hughes's work was held in 2003 at the Conningsby Gallery, London. A retrospective book collection, *Art, Commercial*, was published in 2002, and *Ten Year Itch*, a celebration of the first ten years of Device Fonts, was

1

2

published in 2005. *Yesterday's Tomorrows*, a collection of Hughes's comics work—including collaborations with Grant Morrison, Raymond Chandler, and Tom DeHaven—was recently launched at the Institute of Contemporary Arts in London.

Although Hughes works in many styles across type design, graphic design, and illustration, his vector illustrations routinely show sophisticated use of shape and color to create form and depth, with very little reliance on line. His *sans ligne* style (a reference to the European *ligne claire* style) has been hugely influential and copied widely around the world.

One type of content that many artists have picked up on— hip people hanging out in modern interiors—dates back to Hughes's work on the graphic novel *The Science Service* for Belgium's Magic Strip in 1989, which in turn shows the early influence of the work of *ligne claire* school artists such as Serge Clerc, Daniel Torres, and Ever Meulen.

110

3

Like his sense of style, Hughes's creative methods vary enormously. "Depending on budget and deadline, it'll be anything from delivering a finished piece without any roughs (if the client trusts you!), to a lengthy drawn-out series of sketches, refinements, alterations, and so on," he says.

"Generally, I build a relationship with a client where after time they relax and are happy for me to explore unusual solutions and to surprise them. The trick here, of course, is to not give yourself so much rope you end up hanging yourself. A good client will also be a good sounding board, and be critical in a constructive and helpful manner and get the best out of you."

4

5

1. 48 Car Collector's Case: Limited-edition print from Toybox gallery show.
2. S J: Singer/dancer's personal logo, produced for Deep Need.
3. Mars Girl: Editorial illustration for *Maxim Magazine* (USA).
4. Clouddog: Children's charity logo, produced for Clouddog.
5. *Louche*: Spoof magazine cover for Von Glitschka Design. Originally published in *Crumble.Crackle.Burn.*

Artist profile:
Mike Quon

Country of origin: USA

Primary software: Adobe® Illustrator® CS2, Adobe® Photoshop® CS2, Adobe® InDesign®

Primary fields: Wide variety of media

URL: quondesign.com

A Los Angeles native and longtime New Yorker, Mike Quon is an illustrator and graphic designer greatly influenced by popular culture and his own heritage. His father, Milton Quon, was one of the first Asian-American artists to work for Walt Disney Studios, creating artwork for *Fantasia* and other animated movie classics.

A graduate of the UCLA School of Design, Quon is influenced by Andy Warhol and the Pop artists of the day, and by artist Henri Matisse and graphic designer Paul Rand. A voracious interest in people and street life drew him to New York City, where he joined a thriving art scene and a new era of graphic design that was permeating the visual landscape of marketing.

1

2

1. Graphics for Christmas card featuring a transformation of the yin/yang symbol. *Client: Asian CineVision.*
2. Logo for 28th annual Pan-Massachusetts Challenge bike race to raise funds to fight childhood cancer.
3. Baseball graphic for sports promotion.
4. Personal work: part of a series on New York architecture.

All images © 2007 Mike Quon and Designation, Inc.

"From my roots in Southern California," he says, "I saw the world in bold, forceful colors and big, black outlines for a long time—large, flat color fields. With my logo identity work, I bring my artistic sensibility to the creative process of developing engaging and positive symbols that have staying power. Sometimes I work in a Chinese brush style, and I try to incorporate a lot of freestyle drawing."

Over the years, Quon's work has been seen in advertising and promotional campaigns around the world, from Times Square and the Giants Stadium, to the Summer Olympics in Sydney, the World Cup Soccer in Paris, and a department store in Tokyo.

3

NYC

2008

4

Clients have included Samsung, Chase, Hasbro, American Express, Casio, Pfizer, and Panasonic. His artwork has been published in a variety of publications including *Newsweek*, *BusinessWeek*, *Barron's*, *Sports Illustrated*, *Fortune*, and *Crain's*, as well as in several books and his own books *Non-Traditional Design* (1992) and *Corporate Graphics* (1995), both published by PBC International.

Quon's artwork features in the permanent collections of the Library of Congress, *The New York Times*, the New York Historical Society, and the Wakita Design Museum in Japan. As President and Creative Director of his design firm Designation, Inc., he and his team produce a wide range of projects including recent logos for Pfizer and Dow Corning products, theater posters, identities for a jazz festival, and the nation's largest bike ride fundraiser, as well as campaigns for Unisys, Sanofi-Aventis, KPMG, and Verizon.

Quon says he is able to take his design in many directions. "No matter what we're working on, it's always about communication. You have to understand the client's message and find the best way to visually bring it to life."

Artist profile: Mike Quon

Zeptonn (Jan Willem Wennekes; aka Stinger)

Country of origin: The Netherlands

Primary software: Adobe® Illustrator®, Adobe® Photoshop®

Primary fields: Illustration, character design, toy design, identity design, editorial

URLs: zeptonn.nl, studiopats.nl

Jan Willem Wennekes studied artificial intelligence and philosophy before starting his own design and illustration studio, Zeptonn, in the city of Groningen in the Netherlands. His artwork has appeared in leading design websites such as Threadless, blik, TeeTonic, and SplitTheAtom, as well as in numerous magazines including *Computer Arts*, *Publish*, *Identity*, and *Juxtapoz*. His working space is part of Studio Pats, a Groningen-based artists' collective. A book showcasing his work, *Stingermania*, concentrated mainly on his print design, shirt prints, posters, and canvas prints (2007).

"In my work," Wennekes says, "I try to tell a story—mostly a happy, wacky one. If I can bring a smile to the viewer's face, I am content. Often there is something more to be seen if you look again."

1

2

1. **Monsticle Breakout** poster: personal project.
2. **Outbreak/Population** stickers produced for **Pop Cling** *(popcling.com)*.
3. **Wallcrack/Invasion** wall stickers, produced for **Cut It Out** *(cutitout.nl)*.
4. **Munstre Family Pack**, produced for **PixoPop** *(pixopop.com)*.

All images © 2007 Zeptonn (Jan Willem Wennekes).

114

Wennekes lists among his interests: critters, monsters, color, wacky stuff, simplicity, complexity, sketchbooks, street art, skateboards, fair trade, music, coffee, T-shirts, and philosophy. "When illustration and design is your life, you're always busy with it on some level of cognition," he says. "Just reading a book, watching a movie, or walking down the street can inspire you."

Wennekes has two working methods: one for creating clean vector work, which he simply calls "vector," and one for creating a more loose, illustrative style, which he calls "freedrawing."

In his vector style, he draws directly in Adobe Illustrator, using either the mouse or a graphics tablet. In his freedrawing style, Wennekes begins by drawing ideas and possible compositions in his sketchbook with a Faber Castell pen. He then scans the selected sketches into Adobe Photoshop and cleans up the linework there. "A trick that I often use is to make a new layer with the scan and set it to multiply at 79%," he says. "That way, the lines will look stronger and fatter, but you won't cut out any levels. I then take the image into Adobe Illustrator, where I trace it and start playing with colors."

3

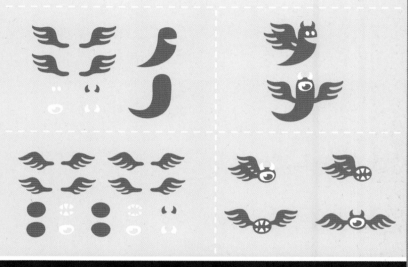

Invasion Creatures
copyright Zeptonn 2007

Of a personal project, the Monsticle Breakout poster (see image 1), Wennekes says, "Every now and then I set out to create a sort of overview piece. I try to use all the techniques that I learned up to that point, and I include illustrations or creatures from other pieces I made." For this piece, he used clipping masks to give each detail its own shade. "Working on such a personal piece is a lot of fun, and often I pick up a few new techniques as well."

4

The
Assembly
Line

6

Flux Capacitor

It has been established that a significant advantage of vector graphics focuses on resolution independence. Including bitmaps in a vector document effectively eliminates that benefit. The realities of a production environment require an application that is flexible enough to handle most design requirements. Providing for the combination of disparate elements creates a document that can be published in many different formats.

Art created in a vector environment can be converted to a bitmap ("rasterized") in a few simple steps. There are several decisions that need to be made as the conversion profile is created. This spread introduces basic decision points that need to be considered to successfully convert a vector into a bitmap.

The vector and the bitmap in review.
At this point, the differences between a vector and a bitmap are clear, demonstrated again by the art above. Vector applications can also convert native art into bitmaps. The process is simple and will vary from environment to environment, but the Adobe Illustrator process is probably the most widely recognized.

118

Document Raster effects setting.
Choosing Object > Rasterize from the menu allows global settings to be assigned. Clicking on the "Use Document Raster Effects Resolution" ensures that all rasterize commands are consistent and eliminates the need for this step every time an object is rasterized.

Rasterize: color model.
The current document will already be set to either an RGB or CMYK document. The color model drop-down will reflect that setting as the first choice. The other two choices, grayscale or bitmap, are always options.

Other options.
The decisions are made for resolution, background, and anti-aliasing, and set using the other controls in the dialog.

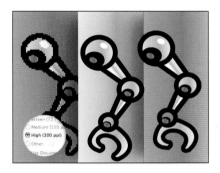

Resolution.
Resolution choices are based on a number of criteria, both technical and creative. Screen resolution, 72dpi, is appropriate for web graphics and multimedia. High resolution, 300dpi, is used for documents that will be commercially printed. 150dpi might be used for a graphic in a PDF file.

Color models.
The current document setting, CMYK for printed documents and RGB for almost all other uses, is the first choice in the drop-down menu and will probably be the choice under ordinary circumstances.

There are generally fewer uses for grayscale and bitmap conversions. Converting to a bitmap might be the least chosen option, but there are creative options for its use.

Anti-aliasing.
Other than as a special effect, rasterizing without anti-aliasing is an unusual choice. Art optimized is best suited for smoothing. Type optimized smooths as well, but uses "hints" to decide how to rasterize text. All fonts have a set of hints that play a role in determining how a font will display on screen, and they are extremely important as the size of the text decreases. Anti-aliasing text with the "type optimized" option chosen should enhance the legibility of rasterized text.

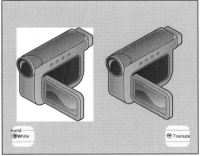

Background options.
Self evident, the options do exactly what the user would expect. The success of the choices depends on technical questions related to the construction of the art. Those questions will be answered in following pages.

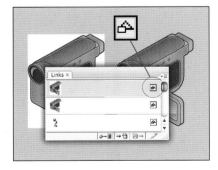

Hints for successful rasterization.
Consider whether the image should be non-destructively (editable) or destructively (permanent) rasterized. There are good reasons for both options. Before a destructive edit is made, make a copy of the object on a separate layer. In the illustration above, the links palette is highlighted with an icon that denotes "embedded." Embedded objects are the result of a destructive edit and are contained entirely in the document (in contrast to linked files covered later).

Vector Mechanics

The decision to convert a vector to a bitmap is based on several factors. File size is probably the most compelling, although there are other situations where conversion might be an advantage. The final publishing environment—such as web, video, or print—is also an important consideration.

In addition to reducing the size of a complex vector document or creating an image using the capabilities of vectors prior to converting to a bitmap, a vector document allows for images of different resolutions to be combined in a single document. This spread includes an example of just that. The first image is a 72dpi graphic. The text is converted at various resolutions and settings, and the sphere on the opposite page is a 300dpi graphic. Another interesting option is combining color images, true grayscale, and 1-bit bitmaps in the same document (see pages 118 and 119, created in Adobe Illustrator). These combinations are not readily achieved in a bitmap editor.

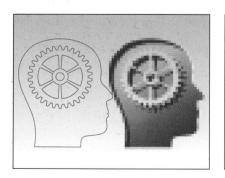

❶ "Greetings," the robot voice said again. The speaker built into the weapon was not the loudest, but the voice was clear. "I sense that I have been captured. I assure

❷ "Greetings," the robot voice said again. The speaker built into the weapon was not the loudest, but the voice was clear. "I sense that I have been captured. I assure

❸ "Greetings," the robot voice said again. The speaker built into the weapon was not the loudest, but the voice was clear. "I sense that I have been captured. I assure

❹ "Greetings," the robot voice said again. The speaker built into the weapon was not the loudest, but the voice was clear. "I sense that I have been captured. I assure

Why convert vectors to bitmaps?
Converting vectors to bitmaps can seem counter-intuitive based on our definition so far (this question will come up again). There are a number of instances where converting to bitmap would be of use: export of graphic to bitmap editor, simplifying extremely complex vector art in a file, or combining the best of a bitmap and the best of a vector and saving the composite result.

Converting live type to pixels.
There are occasions where live text must be converted to a bitmap. In general, the conversion of text sizes (8–14 point) should be avoided. Figures 1–4 above compare the results of various options after conversion to a bitmap. These options are all found in the Object > Rasterize dialog.
1. No Conversion
2. 300dpi conversion, no anti-aliasing
3. 150dpi conversion, type optimized
4. 150dpi conversion, art optimized

120

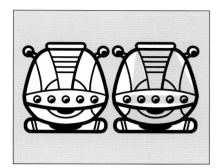

Transparent and opaque options.
The secret of transparency in a vector converted to a bitmap, like the art above left, is closed paths. The art on the right looked fine on a white background. On a colored background, however, unclosed paths left an odd combination of opaque and transparent regions.

Converting a gradient to a bitmap.
Gradients, shape blends, and gradient meshes can often be very complex. Rasterizing them can be the most efficient use of resources, reducing the size of the file and making it faster to open and save.

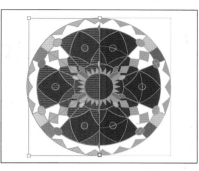

Converting patterns, brushes, and symbols.
Patterns, brushes, and other effects need to be expanded (Object > Expand or Object > Expand Appearance, above left) before rasterized. Expanding converts the object into its component parts (and is a destructive edit). The graphic can then be successfully rasterized (above right).

Color considerations.
Unless a print file uses spot colors, it's a good idea to convert all spot colors to CMYK before attempting rasterization. This is especially problematic in documents with blends: spot-to-spot blend (1); spot to CMYK (2); CMYK to CMYK (3: best option).

Converting complex vectors.
Probably the most complex vector art is the gradient mesh. Rasterizing art created with the mesh is a necessity for many applications (Flash, web, or After Effects) and should be strongly considered for print. The illustration above was Expanded (top left), then Expand Appearance was used. This breaks down a gradient mesh to its most basic components. The right half is the result of a rasterization at 300dpi. This conversion cuts this graphic's size by at least a third.

Colorize 1-bit and grayscale images.
Rasterized black-and-white line work can be colorized. The left side has been rasterized with anti-aliasing and a color applied. The right half of the art is 1-bit (no grays) and is also colorized by applying a color from the color palette.

Outside In

Converting vectors to bitmaps is part of the story of including bitmaps in vector documents. Manipulating, filtering, and significantly altering graphics created in other applications is a strong suit of many vector apps. The difference between an imported bitmap and a rasterized vector is the method by which they are integrated into the document.

Bitmaps can be imported into a vector document in a variety of ways. The method used greatly influences the options available to alter or enhance the imported image.

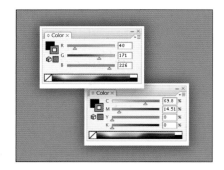

Color space.
While not pertinent in RGB-oriented vector applications, Adobe Flash for example, when the final use is print, the color space is important. CMYK, as discussed earlier, is the color model for printed documents. The application should be set to CMYK when the document is originated. This affects images opened or placed in the document. Without the appropriate setting, undesirable color shifts may occur.

Using File > Open to insert an image.
Bitmap images can be opened as if they are native files of the current application. This is not ideal, but has valuable uses. On the downside, the image embedded in the current file leaves no opportunity for editing in its native application. Embedding also increases the file size, sometimes dramatically. A vector file with an embedded graphic can also cause significant problems if the file is placed in a page-layout application.

The benefits of the embedded file.
When a finished vector file is ready to be printed, an embedded file relieves the designer of searching for and managing linked graphics. Embedded graphics allow access to certain filters that are not available to a linked file. This includes most of the filters available in any bitmap graphics application that supports the Adobe Photoshop plugin format. Some effects and filters are not available to placed graphics.

122

The placed file.
Linking files is the preferred method for including a bitmap graphic in a vector document. A file is placed using the File > Place menu item, checking the "link" button before clicking on "place". This keeps file sizes low and allows for editing the bitmap in its native application, which is then updated in the vector document.

Recognizing embedded images.
Embedded images are designated by the small icon (highlighted above) in the Links palette. A linked file would not have any icon. The links palette is also the place to embed a file that was previously linked.

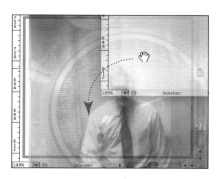

Drag and drop a bitmap.
Most applications support drag and drop as an alternative method to include a bitmap file in a vector document. This is the functional equivalent of copying and pasting a graphic into the vector document. Both methods embed the graphic.

Cut-and-paste.
Cut-and-paste generally require more system resources as it places a copy of the image in the system's clipboard, allowing it to be pasted in multiple documents. As previously indicated, drag and drop or cut and paste both embed the graphic.

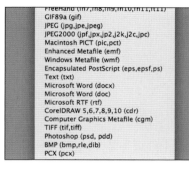

Opening files.
Any number of graphic file formats are supported and can be opened directly. Each of these formats has different properties. Opening them will embed a bitmap that has the properties of the original file. A GIF file can be opened directly, but it has a limited color palette and will be a 72dpi file.

Opening PDF documents.
An emerging standard for distributing files, the Adobe PDF file format can support both bitmaps and vector objects. When opening a PDF, a dialog presents the opportunity to open specific pages in a multipage document. The resolution of the bitmaps can be specified and all vector objects maintain vector status.

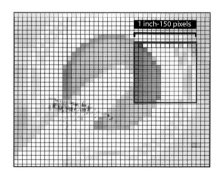

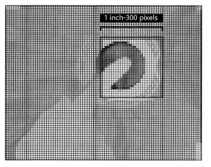

Bitmap resolution, or "Who said I won't need math when I become a designer?".
The resolution of the average monitor (at least in the computer stone age circa 1995) was 72dpi. 72 dots (or pixels) per inch is the resolution of a document intended to be displayed exclusively on screen — a Flash document or a web page. Print requires a 300dpi document or 300 pixels per inch. This means a print file has over 4 times as many pixels per inch than a screen document. The image above on the left is a bitmap with a resolution of 150 pixels per inch and is 4 inches wide. The image on the right is a duplicate of the image on the left, reduced to half the width (from 4 inches to 2 inches). Reducing the physical size (width) increases the number of pixels in an inch—the image is smaller but contains the same number of pixels. A pixel is always the same size. By reducing the image width by half, the number of pixels in an inch doubles. The image on the right is now 300 dots per inch.

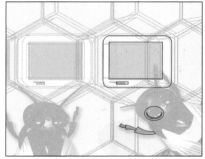

Templates.
Using the Open command and choosing template, a graphic is opened on a layer in your document as an embedded image with decreased contrast. This is a handy tool for scanned pencil roughs that are going to be traced.

Linear Articulation

The overwhelming number of vector filters demands that they be explored with a sense of play. Happy accidents abound in the process, especially when multiple filters are applied to the same object.

Using an original image depicting the dilemma of choosing between (then) two new operating systems—Windows XP and Mac OSX—the illustration was created entirely in vectors using letterforms and typographic symbols. A series of both vector and bitmap effects is applied to the image to provide a basic overview of some of the possibilities.

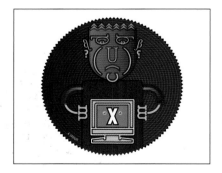

The original vector illustration.

Bulge.

Zig Zag.

Scribble.

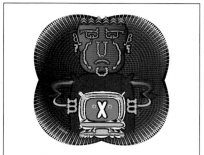

Bloat.

Twist.

Poster Edges.

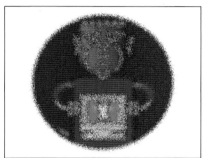

Spatter.

Effect > Texture > Mosaic.

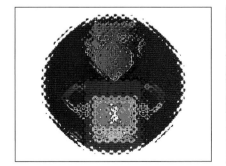

Glass Distortion.

Sponge.

Diffuse Glow and Twist.

Tutorial:

Cause and Effect

Most vector applications allow for some level of bitmap manipulation. Those that focus on print arguably offer the most robust tools for both the destructive and nondestructive use of filters and effects.

Again, using Adobe Illustrator as the primary example, the following is a gallery of filters and effects applied to linked files, embedded files, and vectors.

Placed file.
The original file is placed in the document and linked. Linked files are limited to using primarily the "Filters" menu. Filters are nondestructive, but somewhat limited.

Uses bitmap filters when bitmap is embedded.
Vector art of any type can be used in conjunction with the bitmap. Different filters can be applied to each or a single filter can be applied to both.

Only way to use Adobe Photoshop filter including combine filters in the filter gallery.
A bitmap must be embedded to apply any of the options found in the "Effects" menu. This also allows the use of the "Filter Gallery" and the combination of multiple effects.

126

Patchwork, live.
The patchwork filter, applied "live" or nondestructively.

Create Mosaic, Create a series of vector objects.
The mosaic command can only be applied to an embedded graphic. The number of "boxes" can be controlled.

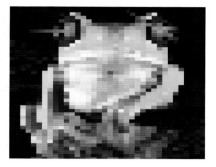

Edit vector objects in Mosaic.
Once applied, the image is a series of vector objects, completely editable. Every piece of the mosaic can be treated just like any other vector object.

Auto-trace black and white, limited palette.
The auto-trace command can be used on any embedded bitmap. The result can be a 1-bit bitmap, a grayscale image, or color. This was auto-traced in black and white with a limited palette.

Auto-trace black and white, 256 grays
(maximum grays).
This is the result of an auto-trace in full grayscale.

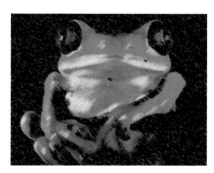

Auto-trace gray, embedded charcoal filter.
Auto-traced in full grayscale with a charcoal filter applied.

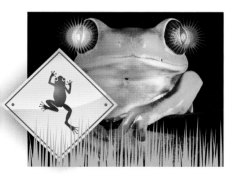

Vector and four-color.
Vectors can be applied to any bitmap image and made to integrate into the image, or left to clearly contrast the hard-edged with the soft-edged.

Auto-trace color.
This is an example of a full-color auto-trace of the embedded image. Compare the resulting vector to step one. The quality is astonishing.

Auto-trace color, global color shift.
Once again, as a vector, the auto-traced image can have any vector filter applied to it. This allows for the use of a feature illustrated here where the color is altered globally and nondestructively.

Tutorial:

Outward Bound

There are many different types of vector and bitmap formats. Some support layers, some support transparency, some are proprietary and required by other applications in specific formats, like the Pixar bitmap format for use in the Pixar Animation System. Different applications support different formats, but the process is essentially the same.

Many of the export options are common to all vector-based applications. The Export option translates the document into formats other than vectors. Save and Save As allow saving to formats that are native to the host program.

Saving.
Saving will generally not offer a dialog box. The file will be saved in the existing format.

Save As or Saving a Copy.
Save As will offer a dialog box with options to choose native file formats. The options here are various vector formats. After saving as, the current document will be the new saved document. Save a Copy will offer the same options, but does not change the current document.

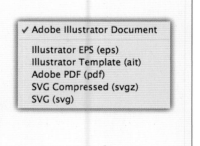

Native file formats.
From Adobe Illustrator, .AI files, .EPS files, and .PDF files are formats that do not require conversion. They are all opened and edited by Illustrator and other apps. A template (.ait) opens as an untitled copy of the original and .svg files, never widely used, are an exchange format that originated as an Adobe Flash "competitor."

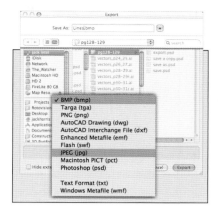

Export common bitmap formats.
.BMP, .JPEG, and .TIFF files are bitmaps with slightly different features. A .BMP is a 32-bit (full-color) PC format. .TIFF supports layers and alpha channels. A .JPEG is probably the most common file format because of its compression capabilities.

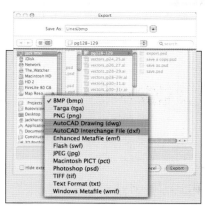

Export specialized vector formats.
AutoCad .DWG files are those read directly by AutoCad, an application used in architecture, construction, and interior design. AutoCad .DXF files are compatible with most 3D applications. This allows drawings made in Illustrator to be repurposed in other applications.

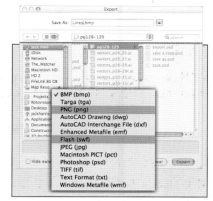

Adobe Flash and other animation applications.
.PNG (pronounced "PING") is a bitmap format best suited for use in Flash. It allows compression and transparency (.JPEG does not support transparency). .PNG files are not yet suited for other uses. Flash (.SMG) files are nearly intact and ready for manipulation in Flash.

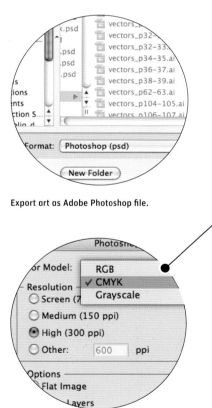

Export art as Adobe Photoshop file.

Similar options in Document Raster Setup.
Determining the size and color space is an important initial decision when exporting to Photoshop.

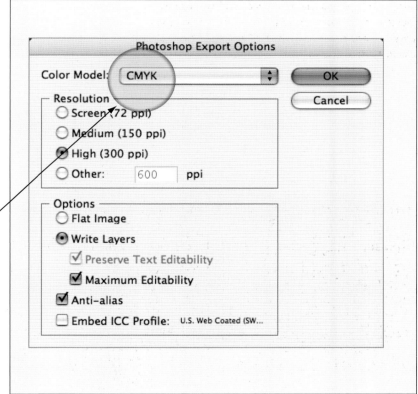

The Photoshop export dialog.
The most powerful feature in the Photoshop export process is the ability to save layers, preserve layer names, and preserve live text in the converted file. This is particularly helpful when saving a file that will need layer-specific effects and filtering or will be saved at some point as a web graphic.

Tutorial:
Beyond Beta

Using a large subset of the available tools, the final **ProtoBot** stands as a shining example of the flexibility and power of vectors. Since the introduction of Adobe Illustrator in 1988, vectors have evolved, emerging as a process, and a format, upon which much of current software is built. Drawing, typography, animation, motion graphics, and even aspects of 3D utilize the concepts and tools that are at the core of much of professional graphic design software today. Even most bitmap editors such as **Adobe Photoshop** and **Corel Painter** rely on vectors as some of their key features.

A career in the visual arts demands expertise in both visual and conceptual thinking and the skills necessary to quickly express those ideas. An expert in the methods and processes presented here has a strong advantage over those less familiar and merely competent with these tools. The best advice, and certainly the most common advice in a visual arts education, is to draw, draw, draw. The same advice is the best advice to master vector drawing.

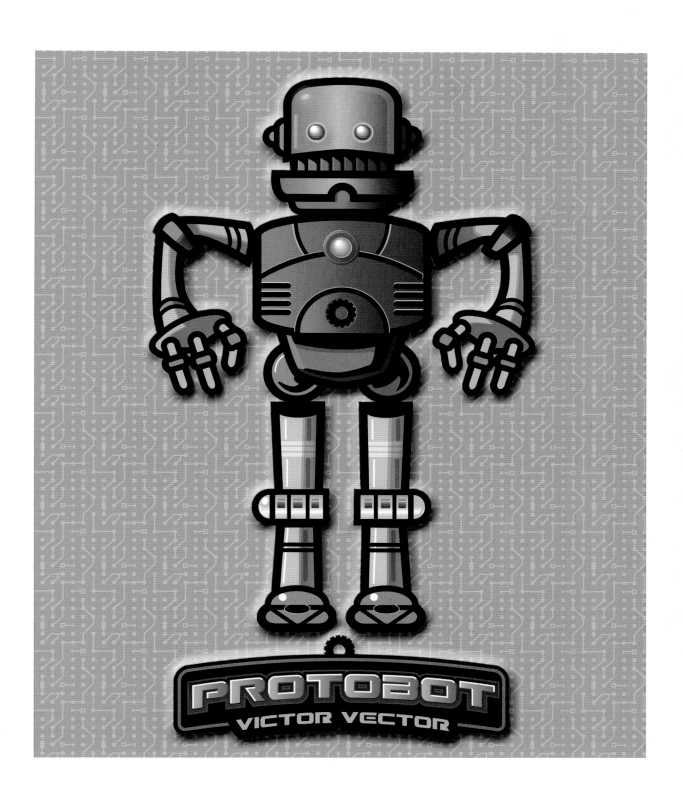

Artist profile:
Petra Stefankova

Country of origin: Slovakia
(now living in UK)

Primary software: Adobe® Illustrator®,
Adobe® Photoshop®

Primary fields: Advertising, editorial,
publishing, animation, 3D

URLs: petrastefankova.com,
yetanotherface.com

Born and raised in Bratislava, Slovakia, Petra Stefankova
moved to the UK in 2006 and now lives in London. She earned
a Master's degree in graphic design at the Academy of Fine
Arts and Design in Bratislava and studied animation at the
Academy of Arts, Architecture, and Design in Prague, Czech
Republic. She won the 4Talent Award organized by British
television company Channel 4 and her clients include the BBC,
Columbia Pictures, Fremantle Media, and others in the UK,
USA, Japan, Australia, and Europe.

1

2

132

Stefankova primarily creates eye-catching, flat, colorful illustrations with "funky and quirky combinations that involve a lot of imagination" for advertising and editorial assignments with quick turnaround times. Her secondary style, branded under the name YetAnotherFace, is a little darker, more mature, and 3D than her 2D work. "It has the quality of classic 3D modeling techniques," she says. "It's more suitable for publishing and any assignments that require a much more artistic, innovative, and experimental approach."

Central to Stefankova's work is her close attention to color composition and structure. "It's similar to playing chess, and it's always helpful if you know how to analyze your pictures and think of every touch as if the finding of balance was a game or a quest," she says. She notes the influence of Russian Constructivism on her thinking in this regard.

"In some cases," she says, "the process can still be intuitive, and this is something brought to me by studying Surrealism. There were situations when I have either chosen the right colors straightaway or I created the picture in a few shades of gray first and the coloring itself was done in Adobe Photoshop. It allowed me to come up with an entirely new palette."

3

1. **Harvest Time: Editorial illustration for the US edition of *Future Music* magazine featuring the Future Music ACE Awards (produced for Future Network).**
2. **Summer in London and Tokyo: Double-page spread for the brochure "What is summer?" produced for Phosphor Art, London.**
3. **Hats, Cats, and Dogs: Illustration mounted on a one-of-a-kind sketchel bag produced for Jeremyville, Australia.**
4. **Christmas: Postcard produced for Phosphor Art, London.**

All images © 2007 Petra Stefankova.

4

Artist Profile: Petra Stefankova

Artist profile:
Charlene Chua

Country of origin: Singapore (now living in Canada)

Primary software: Adobe® Illustrator®, Adobe® Photoshop®

Primary fields: Advertising, editorial, business and product illustration

URL: charlenechua.com

Charlene Chua is an award-winning illustrator from Singapore. Her work has appeared primarily in Southeast Asia, the UK, and Australia, and covers such diverse subjects as retail promotion, real estate, children's comics, CD covers, and even jigsaw puzzles. She now lives in Toronto, Canada, and is part of the illustration group Sketch Motel. She also pursues personal projects such as her graphic novel series. Chua describes her style as "vector-based, stylized illustration with Eastern and Western pop-culture influences."

<u>1</u>

<u>2</u>

She lists among her influences fine artists Alphonse Mucha and Erté; fantasy artists Boris Vallejo and Yoshitaka Amano; pinup artist Alberto Vargas; and comics artists Jim Lee and J. Scott Campbell.

Fond of the gradients and details possible with an airbrush, Chua is able to bring similar techniques to her work in Adobe Illustrator, particularly through the use of masks, but with far more ease and precision than with a traditional tool.

Chua finds drawing the initial sketch to be the most difficult part in creating

134

3

there's no point doing it up in Adobe Illustrator or anything else," she says. While she works primarily in Adobe Illustrator, she often applies final color tweaks in Adobe Photoshop. She also finds that applying noise filters comes in handy in reducing banding issues in gradients.

"In general, I don't use gradient meshes because I find them rather clunky," says Chua. "They definitely have their uses, but for my style, it's more pleasing for me to work with normal gradient swatches."

4

Artist Profile: Charlene Chua

Artist profile:
Ellen McAuslan

Country of origin: UK

Primary software: Adobe® Flash®

Primary fields: Animation (festivals and web), print illustration

URLs: rubberfish.com, fishfoundry.com

After graduating from Middlesex Polytechnic in London with a Bachelor's degree in fine art, Ellen McAuslan started experimenting with scratch animation drawn directly onto film, stop motion, and drawn animation on cells. She survived a short stint as a pop singer before becoming a professional web designer and art director. All the while, she was working in Adobe Flash, which she used in creating her most enduring character to date—Ms Swat.

Ms Swat first appeared as an interactive birthday card, and inspiration led McAuslan to create three short movies with her as the heroine. *Skin Deep* was shortlisted for the Depict! 2001 competition and shown as part of the 2002 Bristol Brief Encounters movie festival.

McAuslan often scans her sketches into Adobe Photoshop and makes composites of the various elements. She imports the resulting composites into Adobe Flash and then traces and draws, gradually working into and simplifying the resulting image. "There are times when things just don't come together, and for me this is the time to come away from the computer again," she says. "The process of correction in the rendering is continuous, so if it's not working out, there is probably something not right in the inherent design. I feel comfortable now with this somewhat cyclical, hands-on process—there's more 'me' in it."

1.   Still from Cold-hearted Beach.
2 & 4. Stills from Sheepscape.
3.   Still from Pneumatic 2.
5.   Still from Skin Deep.

All images © 2007 Ellen McAuslan.

1

2

3

136

When McAuslan started creating web animations, bandwidth was still a big issue, so keeping her style simple and her backgrounds uncluttered was a practical as well as an aesthetic choice. "The prevalence of the color red working against the thick black lines gave a pop-arty, stylized edginess to the cartoons," she says. "After seeing the animations projected on the big screen at a couple of festivals, I realized just how beautifully simple and iconographic the images could be, and I decided to make large prints of my latex heroine."

On the print side, McAuslan has been able to call on her passion for wallpaper patterns. "In the Pneumatic series, they almost compete with the foreground for dominance," she says. "I've used more shading, but the overall effect, though convoluted, is still graphical, and there is a theme of ambiguity in the complexity as well as the simplicity of the Swat prints."

4

5

Artist profile: Ellen McAuslan

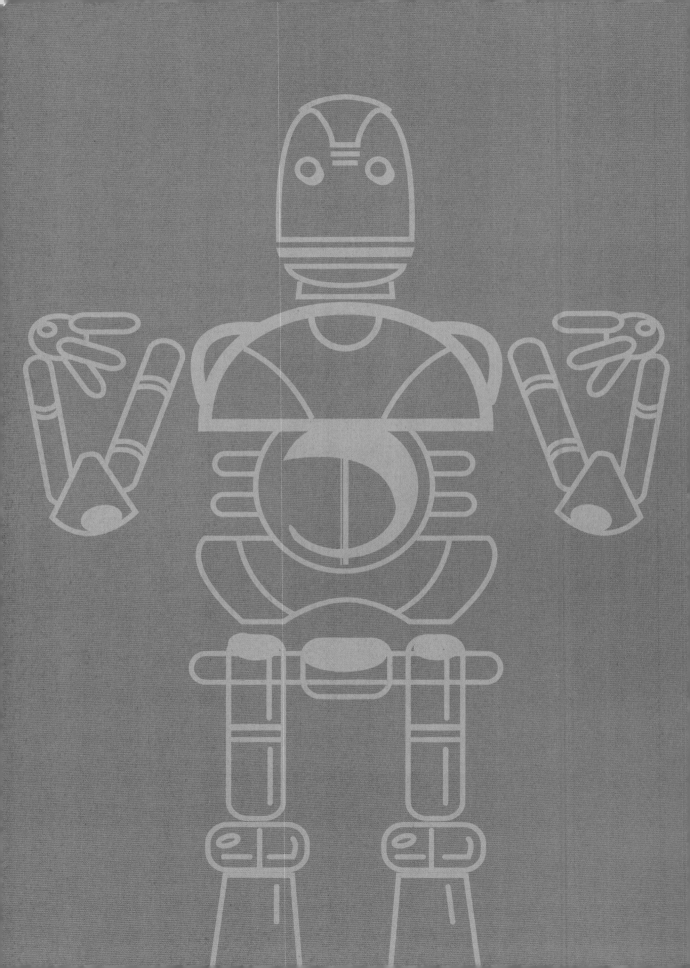

Other Common Applications

7

Vectors in Print

To anyone who has created a "suite" of printed marketing and business identity materials such as stationery, business cards, and fax forms—in which logos, text, or other graphics are frequently manipulated and resized—the benefits of vectors are immediately apparent. Here we asked designer Patrick Coyle (see sidebar) to offer some commentary on a few aspects of vector art unique to print production and printing.

1

2

3

Says Coyle, "You will notice a marked increase in detail on printed pieces that use vector images. Even at very high resolutions, you can usually tell the difference between a pixel-based graphic (also known as a raster image or contone in prepress) and a vector graphic. However, this depends on the type of output: for instance, billboards and other large-scale graphics are not going to look any different up close because the dot patterns on those types of pieces are purposefully increased and are only supposed to be viewed at a distance."

Vectors can also raise the image quality when printing from lower-end laser printers common in many offices and homes. "If you can't afford professional printing services, vector graphics will help your final product look sharper," says Coyle, adding that the most notable increase in quality is when printing directly from vector-editing software rather than from Adobe Photoshop or a web browser.

140

"Whenever a client asks, 'What do you need from us?' the first answer is ordinarily a vector-based version of any design assets, usually the logo," he says. Since they are not married to background colors or images, as raster images are, vector logos can be dropped on multiple different background colors or patterns without worrying about aliasing and transparency issues.

Coyle also points out that the popular program Adobe InDesign now allows designers to import, place, and edit vector graphics within the software. "This allows designers to make edits to the original vector file, often in Adobe Illustrator, and save it without having to save the image out from Illustrator as a .tif, .jpg, or .eps file and then import it back into the layout program."

"If you use Quark XPress as your design layout tool," he adds, "you will have to convert to the rasterized file formats that Quark accepts, and you can't do any layering of those vector graphics on top of other images or colors. That type of image assembly will need to be done either in the vector software where the graphic was created or in a program that can save out Quark-friendly file types."

Patrick Coyle

Patrick Coyle has been a designer for 15 years, working primarily in the interactive field, but also in branding, print, and publishing. He is now the art director for TripAdvisor.com, the world's largest user-based travel review website. Previously, he was an art director for Lycos, a design director for Razorfish, and art director at Molecular, Inc. His client list includes Sony, Bank of America, Fidelity Investments, The Boston Red Sox, Charles Schwab, and Hasbro.

In 2000, Coyle co-founded the online comics publisher Komikwerks.com, which features independent comics created by film, animation, video game, and professional comics writers and artists. In the past seven years, Komikwerks has branched into print with a series of comics anthologies, partnered with comics legend Stan Lee for an online comics subscription service, supplied comics content to the AOL: Red website, and published the Actionopolis line of illustrated prose novels for young adults.

4

1 & 2.   Covers for three Actionopolis titles.

3.   Completely vector-based cover for the Komikwerks Rockets and Robots anthology.

4.   Logo for Actionopolis line of titles, designed by Patrick Coyle.

See page 176 for copyright notices.

Vectors on the Web

Although vector graphics can be output as web-ready graphics such as .gif, .jpg, .png, and .swf (Shockwave Flash) files, or included as part of many different video formats, they cannot be used on their own in HTML (hypertext markup language) for the web. Only three methods are currently used to display vector graphics directly (as opposed to being converted to a bitmap format) over the web: Adobe Flash, Scalable Vector Graphics (SVG), and Microsoft's Silverlight technology.

Adobe Flash (discussed in more detail on pages 152–155) is the standard accepted technology for the display of vector graphics and vector graphics animation on the web. Adobe claims on its website an install base of 99% of web browsers in "mature markets" (i.e., not third world) for the Flash Player version 6 and above.

SVG is an open-source standard adopted by the World Wide Web Consortium (W3C; the group that sets the specifications for HTML, CSS, and other web standards), as a nonproprietary technology somewhat comparable to Adobe's proprietary Flash. Adobe was actually instrumental in developing this technology before acquiring Flash by purchasing Macromedia. A few browsers have native support (built into the browser),

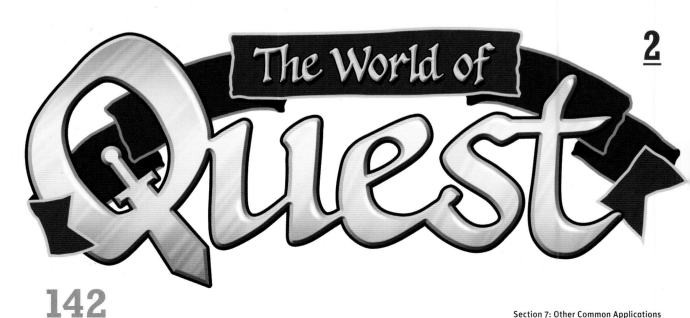

142

3

but it is often partial or incomplete support, and Internet Explorer requires a plug-in. Some argue that SVG has never been widely adopted because of the ubiquity of Adobe Flash. Microsoft Silverlight, an emerging proprietary technology, aims to compete head-to-head with Adobe Flash. According to the Microsoft Developer Network website, "Silverlight is a cross-browser, cross-platform plug-in for delivering the next generation of .NET-based media experiences and rich interactive applications for the web." At the time of writing, it remains to be seen whether Silverlight will catch on with users worldwide to the level that Flash has achieved.

Vectors for web design

Says web designer Patrick Coyle (see pages 140 and 141), "I like to use vector programs for quick layouts, what I call 'gray-boxing.' I use Adobe Illustrator for this. Sometimes when I'm working through a webpage's layout, or the spread for a print piece, I'll establish my grid and work through the final layout this way. Because all the graphics are vector-based, it takes me seconds to create a shape, place it on my grid, and then alter it to fit, if it needs to."

Once all the parts are in the layout, Coyle finds it very simple to move one part, or grab multiple elements, alter them at the same time, or move them at the same time. He can then export this into Adobe Photoshop and use it as a backdrop that establishes his layout grid.

4

5

1. Logo for Komikwerks.com, designed by Patrick Coyle.
2. Logo for the comic The World of Quest, designed by Patrick Coyle.
    The World of Quest © 2007 Jason Kruse.
3 & 4. Homepage and logo for Comics2Film.com, designed by Patrick Coyle.
5. Bookstore page for Komikwerks.com, designed by Patrick Coyle.

Artist profile:
Federico Jordán Gomez

Country of origin: Mexico

Primary software: Adobe® Illustrator®

Primary fields: Editorial, advertising, fine art

URL: fjordan.com

Federico Jordán Gomez is an editorial and advertising illustrator whose work has been published in *Forbes*, *Harvard Business Review*, *The Wall Street Journal*, and *The New York Times*, among other publications. His client list also includes Aeroméxico, American Airlines, Reed Elsevier, Cahners, Lycos, and UNISYS.

Born in Torreón, Coahuila, Mexico, Jordán received formal training as an architect at the Autonomous University of the Northeast and holds a Master's degree in art education from the same institution. He is currently a professor in the School of Visual Arts at the Autonomous University of Nuevo Leon, and lives in Monterrey, Nuevo Leon, Mexico.

1

2

In Jordán's work, there is an emphasis on flat, freehand shapes and organic lines. The noticeable lack of typical "Illustrator blends" and filters gives his art a fresher, almost silkscreen feeling. "I do not like complicated and useless tools in vectors software; I like simplicity," he says.

"When I draw with vectors, I like to respect the expression of my drawings in graphite," he continues. "I draw a lot from my observation and imagination," he continues. "I do not draw directly in the computer without a pencil drawing that is shared with the client and serves as template, but in many cases I solve problems, improvise, and experiment using the vector application along with my template."

In his final artwork, Jordán prefers to use a stroke with a calligraphy brush effect, which makes the final artwork feel warmer and more natural.

Jordán says he enjoys working in a "Robinson Crusoe" mode, setting creative limitations for himself so that he is continually challenged to find the most effective solutions. Fun and spontaneity are important for communication, he says; "they are great tools to create empathy in the audience."

4

3

1 & 3. **Original sketches and final illustrations for two advertisements for CEDIM, a design school in nothern Mexico.**
Reprinted with permission of CEDIM.

2. **Personal work.**
© 2007 Federico Jordán Gomez.

4. **Editorial illustration for Chilango Magazine in Mexico City, about a man who loves technology and gadgets.**
© 2007 Federico Jordán Gomez.

145

Information Graphics

Information graphics, or infographics, are visual explanations of numbers, geography, events, and processes—in short, any data or knowledge—that help readers/users to understand an often complex subject. Simple infographics can be found everywhere from street signs to subway maps. More sophisticated graphics are used as tools across the sciences, in journalism and architecture, and throughout academics—anywhere information needs to be visualized or communicated conceptually.

Diagrams, charts, graphs, maps, and timelines are just a few of the forms information graphics can take. Most use a variety of symbols, icons, and pictograms that can be easily grasped or explained with the help of a legend, scale, or labels, often incorporating text. Digital infographics can include 2D and 3D animation, interactivity, audio, and video.

According to Nigel Holmes, an expert in the field (see profile on pages 148 and 149), the primary principles of information design are clarity, simplicity of form, economy of line, color coding, rejection of decoration, helping comprehension through

contextual examples, and humanity. As we have shown throughout the book, vector graphics can fit most or all of these criteria, and they are often the "go to" choice for information designers.

Case study: Colin Hayes

Designer and illustrator Colin Hayes (colinhayes.com) drew his first paid illustration for a magazine in the Seattle area (where he still lives) shortly after graduating from the Art Institute of Seattle in 1989. "It was done digitally in Aldus FreeHand," says Hayes, who now works in FreeHand MX, but is in the process of migrating to Adobe Illustrator since FreeHand has been discontinued.

According to Hayes, his semitechnical, infographic style emphasizes humor when possible and has a mock "airline safety brochure" look at times. His early work was far more whimsical and far less technical, and he says he fell into the technical style almost by accident after illustrating user guides for Hewlett-Packard deskjet printers for several years.

A PICTURE OF PARANOIA
HERE IS A THREE-DAY HUNT THE AUTHOR MADE LAST SPRING WHERE TRADITIONAL TACTICS FAILED

1

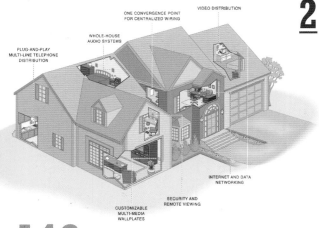

2

Hayes says his work is more illustrative in nature (often involving people, actual settings, real items, and so on) than "traditional" infographics (involving recognizable symbols or icons). "The dimensions of the illustration are important, so I know how much room I'll have to show detail, or lack thereof, to convey the concept," he says.

Hayes prefers a lot of interaction with the art director or client, sometimes sending several rounds of sketches to get more specific feedback. He needs to understand what aspects of the product, system, or idea the client wants him to convey. The level of simplicity in the image also depends on the target audience (general public versus industry insiders, for example).

Hayes generally relies on the client for most of the critical information, and many clients send him documentation, photo references, and/or rough sketches. "Otherwise, I use Google Images a lot, and I shoot a lot of my own photo reference," he says.

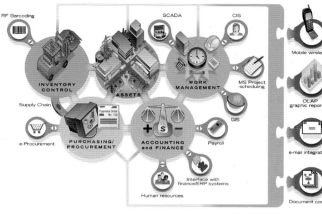

3

4

5

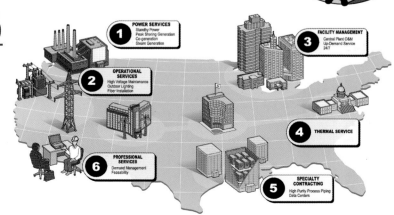

1. Turkey hunt, Field & Stream magazine.
2. Integrated home, Leviton Telcom.
3. Workflow management, Synergen, Inc.
4. Movie piracy, Sound & Vision magazine.
5. Integrated Services, Emcor Energy Group.

All images © 2007 Colin Hayes.

Artist profile:
Nigel Holmes

Country of origin: UK
(now living in USA)

Primary software: Adobe® Illustrator®,
FreeHand MX, Adobe® Photoshop®

Primary fields: Advertising, books, charts
and diagrams, corporate identity, logos,
branding, websites

URL: nigelholmes.com

Nigel Holmes does explanation graphics. He graduated
from London's Royal College of Art in 1966 and worked
as a freelancer for newspapers and magazines in England
until 1977, when Walter Bernard hired him to work at
Time Magazine in New York.

As graphics director of *Time*, his pictorial explanations
of complex subjects gained him many imitators and a few
academic enemies. To this day, he remains committed to
the power of pictures and humor to help readers understand
abstract numbers and difficult scientific concepts.

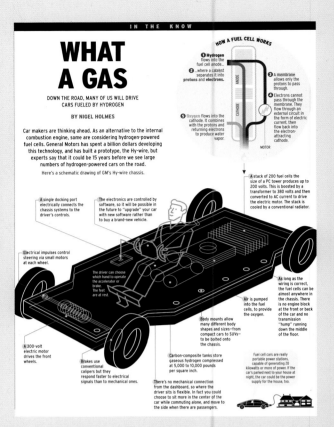

1

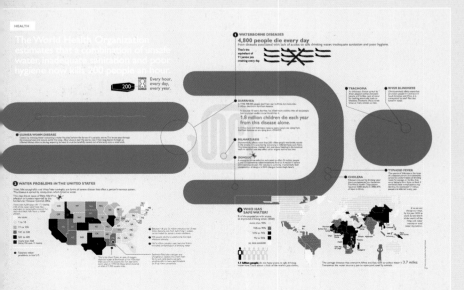

2

1. How a hydrogen-powered car works, from
   Attaché Magazine.
2. Health aspects of the global water crisis,
   from Rick Smolan and Jennifer Erwitt's book
   Blue Planet Run (Earth Aware Editions,
   2007).
3. How to tie a scarf, European style, from
   Wordless Diagrams.
4. Cost of exhibiting at an international art fair
   for Art and Auction, Databank page.
   *All images were created in FreeHand MX and
   converted to Adobe® Illustrator® CS2.*
   © 2007 Nigel Holmes.

After 16 years, *Time* gave him a sabbatical, and he never went back. Now Holmes has his own company, which has a variety of clients, including Apple, Fortune, Nike, Sony, The Smithsonian Institution, United Healthcare, US Airways, and Visa, and he continues to do graphics for publications such as *The Atlantic Monthly*, *The New York Observer*, and *The New York Times*.

Holmes has also written six books on aspects of information design. The most recent, *Nigel Holmes on Information Design* (Pinto Books, 2006), is a book-length interview with Steven Heller. His *Wordless Diagrams* (Bloomsbury USA, 2005) has been published in Chinese, Swedish, and German editions, as well as the original English. "Since there are no words, translation was no problem!"

While 2D graphics remain valuable and versatile for the information designer, both 3D and motion graphics might yet offer even greater possibilities. However, Holmes warns of the risks of indiscriminate usage of these tools. "In many cases, 3D has harmed the practice," he says, "because some artists think that the surface gloss attainable with sophisticated 3D programs is enough to carry a graphic. The look of the graphic becomes more important than the content, and the 'story' that the graphic is telling is lost in a stylistic maze." Holmes adds, "When used properly, 3D can help understanding; when misused, it gets in the way of understanding."

Holmes calls motion graphics "the way of the future," although it has not yet been fully explored. Since many processes are best explained in a sequence (often numbered), he says, motion can take the reader/viewer through these sequences one step at a time, rather than having to see them all at once. And even with otherwise static charts, emphasis can be added, in a cinematic way—for instance, as the numbers in a statistical chart are gradually revealed through time.

"Simple animation techniques are wonderfully suited to explanations," he concludes, "and sound—especially the spoken word—can add a huge amount of explanation potential to motion graphics."

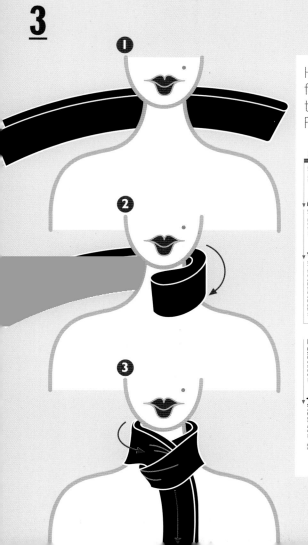

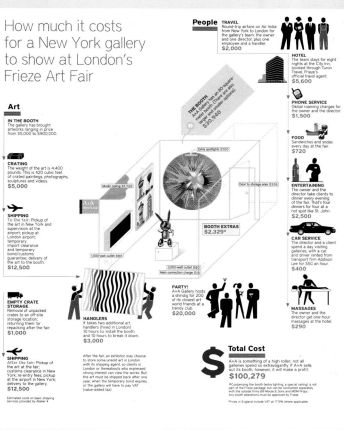

Artist profile:

Dale Glasgow

Country of origin: USA

Primary software: Adobe® Illustrator® CS3, Adobe® Photoshop® CS3, FreeHand 10

Primary fields: Information graphics, print design, identity and brand management

URLs: glasgowmedia.com, daleglasgow.com

A graduate of Virginia Commonwealth University, Dale Glasgow, along with his wife, Sharon, started Glasgow Media in 1985 to serve clients in corporate communications. Glasgow's experience in working for *National Geographic*, *USA Today*, NASA, and many Fortune 500 companies helped to develop his skill for artistic detail. His work can be found in numerous publications and venues including the *National Geographic Historical Atlas*, *Webster's Dictionary*, and the Smithsonian Museum. His studio is located in a country store built in 1900 next door to his family's farm in Hartwood, Virginia.

1

1 There is one teacher

38 villagers are ages 5 to 24

2

150

3

FOOTHILL COUNTRY

4

In 2003, Glasgow was inspired to combine his lifelong interests in history and fine art. The precision and historical authenticity of his work has made him internationally known, as evidenced by his signature painting, *Bird's Eye View of Fredericksburg*, as well as his Jamestown Discovery series of paintings, which can be viewed at DaleGlasgow.com.

As a young artist and painter, Glasgow was influenced by the Hudson River School painters from the 1800s: Frederic Church, Thomas Cole, Jasper Cropsey, Asher Durand, and J.M.W. Turner. "Their work still inspires my landscapes in their artistic depth of creation's beauty and grandeur," he says.

The Bauhaus movement in Switzerland and Germany in the early twentieth century is central to Glasgow's work as a vector and digital artist, particularly the work of Ludwig Mies van der Rohe and László Moholy-Nagy. "Their artistic methods, merged with graphical thought, simplicity of line, and formation of the page is still a standard we work with in today's publishing industry," Glasgow comments.

The "USA Today School" of information graphics, led by Richard Curtis and George Rorick, also influenced Glasgow's early work, as did the work of Nigel Holmes at *Time Magazine* (see pages 148 and 149). In addition, Glasgow says the Works Progress Administration (WPA) artists of the 1930s are a strong influence on his vector work, with their fluid lines, strong lighting, shadows, and dimensionality.

"I believe in showing the world around us to bring the viewer into the frame to experience what they know," says Glasgow. "Foreground, middle ground, and background are always in my formula for visual success."

1. Game board created for Solvay Pharmaceuticals ad.
2. Illustration for a National Geographic textbook for schoolchildren on the earth's growing population.
3. A portion of an illustrated map for an ad campaign for Foothill Transit in Los Angeles.
4. Soil map of Virginia created for the US Department of Agriculture.

All images © 2007 Dale Glasgow.

Vectors and Adobe Flash

First introduced in 1996, Adobe Flash is an authoring tool (and media player) that has become one of the world's most popular programs for animation and interactivity. Flash allows users to create and utilize "symbols"—reusable pieces of content that can be employed again and again without significantly increasing file size. That, and the low file size of vector-based type and images (provided they're not overly complex), keeps file size manageable for delivery over the web. (This is one of the reasons Flash quickly overtook animated GIFs as the standard for web animation.) Flash files use a .swf file extension.

1

While Flash can be used for print projects, the tool is in its native element on the web. According to artist, designer, and teacher Charley Parker (cparkerdesign.com), "Web browsers by themselves don't understand vector information, and Flash is the de facto standard for delivering vector content on the web without translating the vector images into bitmaps. This makes it great for animation and page designs."

Flash is increasingly being used for television animation, both for commercials and for cartoon programming (see coldhardflash.com for examples).

Movie clips
When working for web or CD-ROM delivery, Flash lets you use nested movie clips, in which a bit of repeated motion can be captured as a "movie clip" and then manipulated and further animated like a still object. A car tire, for example, could be animated to roll in a movie clip, and the rolling tire movie clip could be duplicated twice within a movie clip of a car; this,

in turn could be animated to move across the stage. "Carrying the idea further," says Parker, "you could have an animated clip of a driver within the car movie clip, and the car movie clip could be duplicated and repeated at different sizes to create a stream of animated traffic, and so on."

On the downside, Parker says, Flash lacks the pan-and-scan "camera movement" tools of a dedicated animation program such as ToonBoom Studio. Nor does it currently have a system of connecting elements (e.g., "bones") found in many dedicated animation applications that allow, for example, the movement of a character's hand by the animator to automatically reposition the connected arm.

Since Flash is resolution-independent, it can be saved out for any required resolution, as long as the proportions are correct. "Unfortunately," Parker notes, "a lot of the ActionScript programming tricks and nested movie clips that can be utilized for web animation can't be directly used when saving out in QuickTime format for video."

1. Montage of stills from animation for Call Federal Credit Union by Canadian animator XDude (xdude.com).

2 & 3. Stills from various Flash animations by German artist and animator Kathi Käppel (kathikaeppel.de).

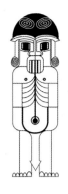
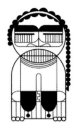

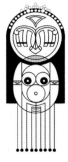

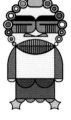

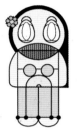

2

3

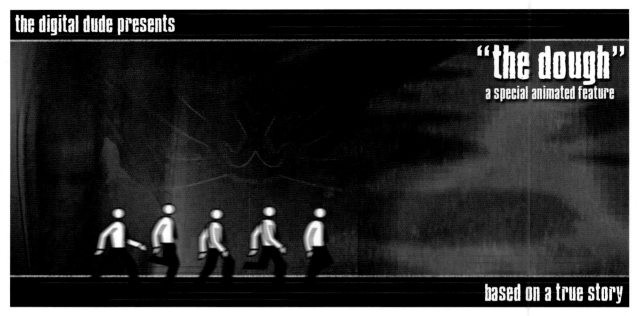

the digital dude presents

"the dough"
a special animated feature

based on a true story

4

Web design and fonts

Says Parker, "The big advantage for nonanimated webpages using Flash is that, unlike bitmapped images, vector images can scale up and down dramatically without loss of image clarity, so the content can be dynamically resized for different monitor resolutions and browser window sizes."

"The other advantage," he continues, "is that Flash can carry font information within the file. This allows the presentation of changeable, dynamic content delivered in font faces that don't necessarily exist on the viewer's computer, a distinct limitation of traditional HTML pages."

The biggest disadvantages in using Flash for actual page design, as opposed to illustration, says Parker, are the issues of difficulty in bookmarking pages within an all-Flash site (though it can be done with some extra scripting) and the inability of search engines to reliably index Flash content, requiring the use of alternative text-based content.

5

"Flash has a reputation for a steep learning curve, and it is perhaps well deserved," Parker concludes. "It introduces concepts that even those experienced in vector-based illustration programs will find unfamiliar. I've learned many graphics applications from books, and taken most of them to an expert level; but of all of them, Flash is the one for which I would have benefited most from taking a class initially."

154

4 & 6.   Stills from the short movie The Dough
         by XDude.
5.   Still from Catfish, a short Flash-animated
         movie by American artist and animator
         Clio Chiang (cliochiang.com).

6

Patrick Coyle on Adobe Flash

When creating a Flash-based site, or a Flash element within a website, you should ask yourself, "Is this animation truly necessary? What benefit does it provide the user?" Consider your audience and the purpose of the website to determine the following:

* Does your audience use the most up-to-date web browsers, and are they likely to download and install drivers and plug-ins? If so, then you're probably safe using Flash. If not, then you might lose some (or all) of your potential audience.

* Is the purpose of your site largely informational? Are users coming to your site to read lots of text and print it out? If so, Flash is not ideal for those purposes.

* Is your site mostly photos that you need to animate and scroll and move around? If so, Flash might be a good option. If you want every element on your site animated, then Flash is most likely a good option.

* If you are going to populate your site using a database of content, Flash can do that, but it is tricky. I would think twice before going that route.

* If your reason for using Flash is, "Because it looks really cool," I would avoid using Flash. It's true that Flash does allow for some great-looking animations and transitions between pages, but it is not always the most user-friendly solution for a website.

* Also, there are other development solutions than can accomplish some of what Flash does. CSS, DHTML, Java, and Javascript all allow for lots of great development tricks and can be implemented in a more conventional and user-friendly way.

(See pages 140 and 141 for more about Patrick Coyle.)

Artist profile:
Alexandru Sacui

Country of origin: Romania (now living in USA)

Primary software: Adobe® Illustrator®, Adobe® Flash®

Primary fields: Flash animation, web, graphic novels, book and magazine illustration

URL: nosepilot.com

Born in Romania and now living in Asheville, North Carolina, illustrator and designer Alexandru Sacui has spent a lifetime making visual art in many media: clay, wood, metal, papier mâché, fabric, stained glass, painting, drawing, printmaking, digital 3D, bitmap, and vector.

Sacui says he is inspired by "grandiose Hollywood production" and "the opulent visual magnificence" of some Japanese anime (particularly Katsuhiro Otomo's *Steamboy*). The subject of his art tends to be fantastical, and the color palette is often unrealistic and bright.

1

2

"Unlike independent film, which tends to show the beauty of ordinary life," he says, "Hollywood at its best invents impossibly powerful giants to run though excessively complex surroundings causing mayhem so spectacular it forces awe. I love to see sets, props, and visual effects that appear to have been created by crews of hundreds."

In 1999, Sacui created a seven-minute Adobe Flash animation (drawn in Adobe Illustrator) as a portfolio piece to launch his freelance illustration career. It quickly became very popular and brought heavy traffic to his website for the first few years. In 2002 and 2003, he continued the plot of the animation through a 117-page graphic novel told entirely in images. "The beauty of a vector illustration," Sacui says, "comes not

156

from how convincingly colors are blended, but from the quality of the outlines of the colors." When he started working in the medium, he practiced "severe restraint" and attempted to illustrate with as few colors as possible, concentrating instead on the subtlety of the curves. From the process, a "rather presentable, clean, slick look" emerged.

Sacui has shied away from exploring more complex, fully shaded compositions because of what he perceives as the "unattractive, sloppy look of unblended vector brush strokes." Recently, however, he has begun to use some gradients, transparencies, and blurring, though he still pays close attention to the outline of each color. "In painting," he says, "quick, fevered brush strokes can look vibrant. The naked mark of a brush has its own beauty. Quick marks made with a mouse in a vector program look extremely awkward."

Sacui is continually challenged by the painterly vector style of Russian artist LimKis (limkis.com), who, he says, "ignores the graceless nature of raw, unrefined vectors and piles them together into overall beauty."

"I still lack her courage," he sighs.

1. Page from unpublished graphic novel.
2. Poster for Asheville band Brushfire Stankgrass.
3. Magazine illustration for Florida Association of Realtors.

All images © 2007 Alexandru Sacui.

3

Pictorial Narratives

Given the inherent simplicity and flexibility of vector art, it is no surprise that many thousands of visual storytellers and character designers around the world have come to embrace vector techniques in the fields of animation, comic strips, comic books, graphic novels, manga, *bandes dessinées*, webcomics, and children's picture books.

1

Vector comics

Now having the option of serializing through the web, many cartoonists have chosen to work completely digitally, never putting ink on paper. One up-and-coming online comic strip, *Sheesh* by Jim Keplinger and Steve Musgrave (moderntales.com/comics/sheesh.php), is drawn and lettered entirely using vector software.

2

3

Says Keplinger, "When I letter a strip, I work solely in Adobe Illustrator CS3, as it allows me to rewrite on the fly to make sure we're producing a very consistent product. If Steve [Musgrave] were to be drawing the strips on boards or if I were to be lettering by hand, there would be small inconsistencies when merging hand-drawn art and vector art. By both of us working with the same tools, our strip can be judged on the merits of its art and writing, not how well we fuse two mediums." Working in vectors also allows Keplinger and Musgrave to manipulate the characters and their setting: to change the order of the word balloons, to move objects around the panel, or to add or remove elements completely.

"Resizing is also done quite often," Keplinger says. "For example, in the original script of Episode 8, I wrote three panels and a much shorter conversation. By the time I was done writing the rant in panel 2, the scene had to be shrunk by half and the characters reversed. If we were working pen-and-paper, this would have meant a complete redraw. However, as it was vector, we were able to move the characters where they needed to be, and the rant fit perfectly … and the strip is much better for it."

Chickengirl and children's books

Children's illustration is the perfect playground for Jannie Ho's vivid imagination. Born in Hong Kong and raised in Philadelphia, Ho (aka Chickengirl; chickengirldesign.com) moved to New York City to study illustration at Parsons School of Design. After working as a graphic designer at Nickelodeon and Scholastic, and as an associate art director at *Time* [*Magazine*] *For Kids*, Ho decided that illustration was her true calling and began creating humorous digital illustrations for the children's publishing industry.

Much of her work and style has been inspired, she says, by Japanese packaging design and comic books. Among her favorite vector artists are J. Otto Siebold, Chip Wass, Meomi, and Juliana Pedemonte of Colorblok.

"I try to give my work an organic and hand-drawn look whenever possible, avoiding the cold, mechanical quality that is sometimes felt in digital work," says Ho, who works primarily in Adobe Illustrator. Sterling will publish a Halloween picture book of hers in 2008, and she is also working with Scholastic on a set of emergent reader books, also scheduled for 2008.

1 & 2. Self-promotional projects by Jannie Ho.
        Images © 2007 Jannie Ho.
3.   Strip from online comic strip Sheesh™
        by Jim Keplinger (writer and letterer)
        and Steve Musgrave (artist).
4.   Cover image from The Penguins' Perfect
        Picnic written by Tish Rabe, illustrated by
        Jannie Ho. *(Innovative Kids, 2007)*

Artist profile:
Russell Tate

Country of origin: UK
(now living in Australia)

Primary software: Adobe® Illustrator®

Primary fields: Editorial, advertising,
logos, layouts

URLs: mt-generator.com.au, russelltate.com

Born in Hitchin, Hertfordshire, UK, Russell Tate was a freelance designer in London in the 1980s, working on record sleeves and music magazines using nondigital tools. In 1990, he moved to Sydney, Australia, to be art director for *TV Hits* magazine and was introduced to computers for the first time. "I started doing club flyers in my spare time using Quark XPress and was advised that Adobe Illustrator might be a better application to use," he says.

In the mid-1990s, Tate started a design business, under the name MT GENERATOR, with his wife, who is a fashion stylist. Illustration work takes up most of his time, but he still enjoys logo creation and designing layouts. His client list includes McDonalds, Coca-Cola, Volkswagen, Telstra, Optus, and Amber Bitter Beer, among others.

1

2

"I think most of what I produce I'd call 'cheerful retro,'" he says. "I don't feel I have one particular style, but I do approach most illustrations with a set of rules I impose on myself. Limited color palette in muted tones, simple vignettes and blends wherever possible, simple linework, etc. I don't really think about it now; I just do it without even thinking, like cleaning my teeth or wearing a seat belt in the car."

Tate nearly always starts by drawing in pencil on a sheet of tracing paper. "I prefer tracing paper, as I sometimes adapt a sketch as I'm developing it and may try a new head or eyes on a fresh sheet of tracing paper laid over the top," he says. A finished sketch might exist on four sheets of paper before he does a final master trace.

160

Tate scans the completed sketch into Adobe Illustrator, sizes it, ghosts it back to 50%, and locks it down on a separate layer. The ghosting is done, he says, so that he can trace over the top of the scan with the pen tool and not be confused by the lines of the scan underneath (they will be gray, while the line he is drawing will be black).

"I always use the pen tool, as it's clean and hard-edged, which is the look I like best," says Tate. "I trace the sketch nearly line for line so that the finished illustration has a hand-drawn feel about it still. If I try to draw directly on screen, things look too boxy and geometric."

1. Email spam illustration for front cover of the Sydney Morning Herald's Icon Magazine.
2. Illustration for Battling Buccaneers (interactive game) for Blockbot Inc. (kewlbox.com).
3. Louis Armstrong promotional poster for Soul and Swing CD for Drawing Book Studios/Gary Horner, Whybins TBWA, and the Sydney Morning Herald.
4. Kids height chart for Nasonex and Drawing Book Studios.

All images © 2007 Russell Tate.

4

3

Adobe After Effects

Adobe After Effects, a digital compositing program, is used for special effects, animation, and editing. It contains features from many programs; it can manipulate and create bitmap images, video footage, and vector artwork.

After Effects was created as a digital version of the multi-plane camera. Not only does it have a nonlinear editing system (common to all video-editing programs), but also footage, pictures, drawings, and text are controllable on separate, overlapping layers.

One method for creating vector art in After Effects is the solid. A solid is similar to a piece of paper that After Effects generates. It can be scaled to any size and be made into nearly any shape imaginable. The After Effects tools used to cut up solids are very similar to the tools in Adobe Illustrator: the pen, direct-selection arrow, rectangle, and paintbrush. While strokes and gradients are not native to After Effects, they can be created with some inventive workarounds.

1 & 4.   Images from the music video Three Cheers for the Invisible Hand by Canadian Invasion and Melindathemartian.

2 & 3.   Images from the Midway Pictures studio ID. Constructed from solids, vector graphics, and bitmap files arranged in a 3D space.

All images © 2008 Melinda Rainsberger.

162

Every new solid is displayed as a new layer. However, imported images can be single or multiple layers, depending on what program created them. For vector images made outside After Effects, paths will always import as a flattened image and a multilayer document can be imported flattened or with its layers intact. Merged images are imported as "footage," and multilayer documents are imported as "compositions." The layers will retain their order from Adobe Illustrator, but can be switched later in After Effects. Vector images will retain their vector information, meaning their resolution can be increased for film productions or decreased for web broadcasts with no loss in quality.

In After Effects, vector information has additional uses. The paths of an object can be used as a guide for motion. With both your vector and After Effects programs open, the path for a circle can be copied and pasted into the movement (or position) information of another object in After Effects. This will make the object appear to go around a circle on the "invisible" path. This shortcut can save considerable time when you are working with many layers and need fluid motions.

Additional Resources

8

Reference Guide

Print Resources

Magazines

Adobe Illustrator Techniques (illustratortechniques.com)
Applied Arts (appliedartsmag.com)
CMYK Magazine (cmykmag.com)
Communication Arts (commarts.com)
Computer Arts (computerarts.co.uk)
Create (createmagazine.com)
Creative Quarterly (cqjournal.com)
Desktop (Australia; desktopmag.com.au)
Eye Magazine (eyemagazine.com)
Giant Robot (giantrobot.com)
Grafik (grafikmagazine.co.uk)
Graphis (graphis.com)
Hi Fructose (hifructose.com)
HOW (howdesign.com)
IdN Magazine (Hong Kong; gingkopress.com/_cata/_grap/
   idnmag.htm)
Juxtapoz (juxtapoz.com)
Layers Magazine (layersmagazine.com)
Print (printmag.com)
STEP inside design (stepinsidedesign.com)
Super7 (super7store.com)
3x3 Magazine (3x3mag.com)
Vektorika (vektorjunkie.com)

Books

Adobe Flash CS3 Professional Bible, Robert Reinhardt
   and Snow Dowd (Wiley, 2007)
*Crumble.Crackle.Burn: 120 Stunning Textures for Design
   and Illustration*, Von Glitschka (How Books, 2007)
Digital Illustration: A Master Class in Creative Image-Making,
   Lawrence Zeegen (RotoVision, 2005)
Flash CS3 Professional Advanced for Windows and Macintosh,
   Russell Chun (Peachpit Press, 2007)
*Flash CS3 Professional for Windows and Macintosh (Visual
   QuickStart Guide)*, Katherine Ulrich (Peachpit Press, 2007)
Foundation Flash CS3 for Designers, Tom Green and David
   Stiller (friends of ED, 2007)
How to Draw and Sell Digital Cartoons, Leo Hartas (The Ilex
   Press/Barron's Educational Series, 2003)
*Illustrator CS3 for Windows and Macintosh (Visual QuickStart
   Guide)*, Elaine Weinmann and Peter Lourekas (Peachpit
   Press, 2007)
*Information Graphics: Innovative Solutions in Contemporary
   Design*, Peter Wildbur and Michael Burke (Thames &
   Hudson, 1999)
*Instant Graphics: Source and Remix Images for Professional
   Design*, Chris Middleton and Luke Herriott (RotoVision,
   2007)
Logo-Art: Innovation in Logo Design, Charlotte Rivers
   (RotoVision, 2008)
*Logo, Font, and Lettering Bible: A Comprehensive Guide to the
   Design, Construction, and Usage of Alphabets and Symbols*,
   Leslie Cabarga (How Design Books, 2004)
Nigel Holmes on Information Design, Steven Heller (Jorge Pinto
   Books, 2006)
Real World Adobe Illustrator CS3, Mordy Golding (Peachpit
   Press, 2007)
*Secrets of Digital Illustration: A Master Class in Commercial Image-
   Making*, Lawrence Zeegen (RotoVision, 2007)
The Adobe Illustrator CS3 WOW! Book, Sharon Steuer (Peachpit
   Press, 2007)
The Complete Guide to Digital Illustration, Steve Caplin,
   Adam Banks, and Nigel Holmes (The Ilex Press/Watson-
   Guptill, 2003)
3D Toons: Creative 3D Design for Cartoonists and Animators,
   Steve Anzovin and Raf Anzovin (The Ilex Press/Barron's
   Educational Series, 2005)
Toon Art: The Graphic Art of Digital Cartooning, Steven Withrow
   (The Ilex Press/Watson-Guptill, 2003)
Webcomics: Tools & Techniques for Digital Cartooning, Steven
   Withrow and John Barber (The Ilex Press/Barron's
   Educational Series, 2005)
Wordless Diagrams, Nigel Holmes (Bloomsbury USA, 2005)

Web Resources

Flash animations
AtomFilms (atomfilms.com/films/flash_cartoons.jsp)
Cold Hard Flash (coldhardflash.com)
Flash Showcase (adobe.com/cfusion/showcase/index.cfm)
I Want My Flash TV (iwantmyflashtv.com)

Tutorials
actionscript.org
flashkit.com
flashmagazine.com
illustrationclass.com
kirupa.com
lynda.com (fee-based)
texturebook.com
webmonkey.com

Vector software
Adobe® Flash® (adobe.com/products/flash)
Adobe® Illustrator® CS3 (adobe.com/products/illustrator)
Autodesk AutoCAD (autocad.com)
CorelDRAW (corel.com)
Genuine Fractals 5 (ononesoftware.com/)
Inkscape (inkscape.com, open source)
Microsoft Silverlight (microsoft.com/silverlight)
Silhouette Online (silhouetteonline.com)
Skencil (skencil.org, free)
Synfig (synfig.com)
VectorMagic (vectormagic.stanford.edu, open source)
Xara Xtreme (xaraxtreme.org, open source)

Weblogs/Communities
Art Talk (arttalk.theispot.net)
Cartoon Brew (cartoonbrew.com)
Drawn! (drawn.ca)
Graphics.com
illosaurus.com
Illustration Friday (illustrationfriday.com)
Illustration Mundo (illustrationmundo.com)
istockphoto.com (vector forums)
lines & colors (linesandcolors.com)
Mike's SketchPad (sketchpad.net)
Real World Illustrator (rwillustrator.blogspot.com)
Sugar Frosted Goodness! (sugarfrostedgoodness.com)
Vector Art (vector-art.blogspot.com)
Vexels.net

Associations
AIGA (aiga.org)
Graphic Artist Guild (gag.org)
Society of Children's Book Writers and Illustrators (scbwi.org)
Society of Illustrators (societyillustrators.org)
Society of Publication Designers (spd.org)
ICON The Illustration Conference (theillustrationconference.org)

Glossary

ALIGNMENT AND DISTRIBUTION
Alignment is the process of aligning multiple objects to a single point. The distribution command spreads objects evenly across a specific distance.

ALPHA CHANNEL
In a bitmap editor, an alpha channel is a grayscale layer, separate from the image layers, that is used to create a mask.

ANCHOR POINT
Any point on a Bézier path. A line will have at least two anchor points on either end.

ANIMATION
Rapid display of a sequence of related images to create the illusion of movement.

ANTI-ALIASING
Technique of minimizing the distortion artifacts along the edges of objects, known as aliasing. Commonly known as "jaggies."

APPEARANCE
A feature specific to Adobe Illustrator; a series of attributes such as color, stroke, or effects are defined as a style. This style (appearance) can be applied to multiple objects to speed up production.

ART NOUVEAU
International style of art and design of the late nineteenth and early twentieth centuries characterized by stylized, curvilinear forms often incorporating floral and natural motifs.

BANDING
The result of too few or too many steps in a blend or gradient, resulting in dramatic horizontal lines running through the gradient. This is affected primarily by the length of the gradient and the number of color steps necessary to create the blend.

BAUHAUS
Influential German school (1919–1933) of fine arts, crafts, and architecture founded by Modernist architect Walter Gropius.

BÉZIER CURVE/PATH
Mathematically defined line consisting of anchor points and control points.

BITMAP EDITOR
Computer program such as Adobe Photoshop used primarily to create and manipulate pixel-based graphics.

BITMAP GRAPHICS
Also called rasters or contones (rarely used, short for continuous tone). Resolution-dependent image defined as a grid of differently colored pixels.

BOUNDING BOX
Imaginary box surrounding a selected area.

CLIPPING PATH
A Bézier path that creates a hard-edged mask.

CLOSED PATH
Enclosed Bézier path that has no beginning and no end.

CMYK
Subtractive color model (short for cyan, magenta, yellow, and key [black]) used in most color printing. Often called "process color" or "four color."

COMICS
Graphic form, also called sequential art, manga, and bandes dessinées, in which a sequence of static images, often incorporating text, is arranged in space to convey a narrative or idea.

COMPOSITING
Combining visual elements from separate sources into single images.

COMPOUND PATH
A compound path is the intersection of one or more closed paths. These multiple paths form a single path and can only have a single set of attributes such as color.

CONTROL POINT
Point that is part of an anchor point, used to control the curve of a path.

CORNER POINT
An anchor point that closes an open shape.

CORNER RADIUS
The radius of a curve at the corner of any object.

DESTRUCTIVE/NONDESTRUCTIVE EDITS
Destructive edits are changes made to the art that are permanent when the file is saved. Nondestructive edits can remain editable throughout the life of the art.

168

DIRECT SELECTION
A term that describes the tool and the process of selecting a subset of the parts of an object or a group of objects.

DISPLAY TYPE
Typically describes type used for headlines and type over 14 points.

EDITORIAL ILLUSTRATION
Art and graphics used to summarize a subject or put forth an idea found in magazines, newspapers, and other publications (including certain digital media).

EPS
Encapsulated PostScript file. Standard cross-platform image format based on the PostScript printer language. An EPS can contain vectors, bitmaps, or both, and is a format that can be used in any page layout program. It saves a standard bitmap preview image within the file.

FILL
Attribute that determines color, gradient, or pattern, ideally within a closed shape.

FILTER
A function for special effects. Apply a filter to artwork to achieve many different looks that would be difficult or impossible with vector drawing techniques. There is a concern over excessive use of filters creating artwork that is too complex to output.

FONT
A set of characters in a specific type-face, at a specific point size, and in a specific style. "12-point Times Bold" is a font—the typeface Times, at 12-point size, in the bold style. Hence "12-point Times Italic" and "10-point Times Bold" are separate fonts.

GIF, JPEG
GIF (Graphic Interchange Format) and JPEG (Joint Photographic Experts Group) are image file formats that are universally accepted and supported by all web browsers. GIF files are particularly well suited for graphics with large areas of solid color. JPEG files are intended for photographs or images with wide variations of color. JPEG files can be compressed and make very small files.

GRADIENT
An object fill that contains two or more colors blending smoothly into each other.

GRADIENT MESH
Allows the user to create elaborate shading by plotting colors to each of the intersections of an imaginary mesh so that the colors all blend together.

GRADIENT SWATCH
A graphic in the Swatches palette (Adobe Illustrator) that represents a previously created gradient.

GROUP
Collection of separate objects that can be easily selected, edited, and transformed as if one object.

HTML
Hypertext Markup Language. Describes structure of text-based information in a webpage along with interactive forms, embedded images, and other objects.

INFORMATION GRAPHICS
Also called infographics or explanation graphics. Visual explanations of numbers, geography, events, and processes—in short, any data or knowledge—that help readers/users to understand an often complex subject.

INSTANCE
An instance is conceptually similar to an alias in the operating system. An alias is a very small file and is not the object itself; rather, it is a reference to the original. Instances simply point to a previously created symbol, telling the computer "place a copy of this graphic here" and do not repeat the code describing the object. This allows for large-scale repetition of an object (such as trees in a landscape) without excessively large file sizes.

INTERPOLATION
In vectors, interpolation is the creation of objects between two or more objects to create blends, shape changes, or both. It is similar conceptually to inbetweens.

JPEG
See GIF.

KERNING
Process of adjusting the spacing between two individual letters (see Tracking).

KEYFRAME
Major frames in an animation that represent the beginning and end of a smooth transition. Creating frames between keyframes is called tweening and the resulting frames are called inbetweens. In animation, the lead animator creates the keyframes and an individual referred to as an "inbetweener" creates the other frames.

LAYER
A function within illustration software that allows the user to organize the drawing. As an example it would be likely to see a drawing with layer names such as background, middle ground(s), and foreground. Simply an organizational aid, layers are recommended for easy selection and isolation of objects to facilitate efficient editing.

LEADING
Measurement, in points, describing the vertical spacing between the baselines of at least two lines of type.

LIGNE CLAIRE
"Clear line" style pioneered by Hergé, Belgian cartoonist and creator of The Adventures of Tintin, in which shading is absent and all lines have the same thickness and importance.

LINE ART
Artwork made of solid black and white with no continuous tones or grays.

LOGO
Graphic element, usually associated with a name or descriptor, that forms a visual representation of a company, product, or service. Also referred to as a mark, bug, or symbol. A logo developed with only creative use of typography, traditionally called a logotype, is referred to as a wordmark in contemporary design vernacular.

MASK
A graphic designed to hide and/or show an underlying graphic. White in a mask is "clear," and black is "opaque."

METAFILE
Digital file format that contains both vector and bitmap elements. Specific to Microsoft Windows.

MICROSOFT SILVERLIGHT
Browser plug-in that allows web applications to be developed with features such as animation, vector graphics, and audiovisual playback.

MINIMALISM
Movement in various forms of art and design where the work is stripped down to its most fundamental features.

MOTION GRAPHICS
Graphics using video and/or animation to create the illusion of motion or transformation. Refers to graphics for television and film.

MULTIPLY
Placing one graphic on top of another, creating an effect where the result is the multiplication of the colors, saturation, and opacity of the two. Red set to multiply on top of blue will create a purple.

OBJECT
See Shape.

OPACITY
See Transparency.

OPACITY MASKS
A transparency mask in the form of a bitmap, used in a vector application to create masks that utilize soft edges and gradients (see Clipping Path).

OPEN PATH
Bézier path with unconnected endpoints.

PALETTE
Small interface window that contains iconic references to stored attributes such as colors or fonts.

PATHFINDER TOOLS
Tools (referred to as Pathfinders in Adobe Illustrator, but available in most vector applications) that are used to merge, cut holes, create shapes from intersecting objects, or divide overlapping shapes into multiple shapes, among others. In 3D applications, the same functions are called "Booleans."

170

PDF
Adobe Portable Document Format file. Quickly becoming a standard for sharing and distributing files for review, proofing, legal documents, and consistent printed output.

PEN TOOL
The primary drawing tool in a vector program. The pen tool allows the user to position anchor points and control the shape of a line. The shape can be further refined by manipulating control handles that extend from the anchor points.

PHOTOREALISM
Modern genre of visual art, of which Chuck Close was a leading figure, stressing exact, photographic, sometimes hyperrealistic, detail.

PIXEL
Picture element. The smallest graphic unit that can be displayed on the screen, usually a single-colored dot.

PIXELATED
Usually the result of physically enlarging an image, individual pixels are visible. Considered an undesirable result.

PLUG-IN
Small snippet of code that provides a web browser with functions not native to the browser. Also refers to small programs, similar in concept, that provide added functionality to an application such as Adobe Photoshop.

PNG
Portable Network Graphic. A digital file format, pronounced "ping," used for lossless compression when displaying images on the web. PNG files have the advantage of millions of colors and anti-aliased background transparency. PNG images are not universally supported by web browsers, limiting practical use.

POINT
See Anchor Point.

POP ART
Visual art movement emerging in the 1950s that draws its themes from popular mass culture such as advertising and comic books.

POSTSCRIPT
An industry standard developed by Adobe Systems. PostScript is a page description programming language used to create documents and graphics that are device-independent.

PRIMITIVE
Most commonly refers to premade objects in 3D applications such as ellipses, rectangles, irregular polygons, pyramids, and other commonly used basic shapes. See also Vector Graphics.

RASTERIZATION
Conversion of a vector image to a bitmap. Hardware processing or exporting a digital file into a raster or bitmap. Also referred to as "RIP" (raster image processor): "The file needs to be ripped before it can be printed."

RESOLUTION
Number of pixels in a unit of measure. Generally expressed in pixels per inch (ppi) for printed images or dots per inch (dpi) for screen images.

RGB
Additive color model in which red, green, and blue light are added together in various ways to reproduce a broad array of colors. The presence of all colors at full saturation creates white. Conversely, the complete absence of all three colors is black.

SANS LIGNE
Use of shape and color to create form and depth, with very little reliance on line. See Ligne Claire.

SCALABILITY
The characteristic of an object, such as a vector, to be successfully enlarged without loss of quality.

SEGMENT
A portion of a path between two anchor points. The smallest possible component of a path.

SHAPE
Interchangeable with the term "object" in vectors, it is any element in a vector drawing. Most often used to represent elements created by a closed path.

SHAPE BLEND
Interpolating between two or more shapes to create evolving shapes and colors.

STROKE
User-applied attribute that determines the style of an object's outline.

STROKE WEIGHT
Thickness (width) of a line measured in points. A point is a traditional unit of measure in design. One point is equal to 1 pixel in measurement.

STYLE
A style is a collection of attributes, color, effect, stroke characteristics, that can be saved and easily reused.

SURREALISM
Revolutionary cultural movement begun in the early 1920s that features dreamlike imagery and unexpected juxtapositions, René Magritte being one of the major figures in the movement.

SVG
Scalable Vector Graphics. Open-source standard adopted by the World Wide Web Consortium as a nonproprietary technology somewhat comparable to Adobe's proprietary Flash.

SWATCH
A small graphic icon that represents a default or user-defined color, pattern, or gradient, stored in the Swatches palette in Adobe Illustrator.

SYMBOL
Reusable content, symbols are an instance of a symbol or a "pointer" to the original graphic—not a copy. Can be used without significantly increasing file size to create repeated graphic elements, such as trees in a landscape. See Instance.

TEXTURE OR TEXTURE MAP
Bitmap image applied to a surface in computer graphics, particularly 3D graphics.

THUMBNAIL
Small preparatory sketch drawn to establish layout and composition.

TIFF
Tagged Image File Format. Compression-capable format that is a standard on both Macs and PCs. A TIFF is a bitmap file and is resolution dependent.

TRACING
Using a function available in many vector applications to transform a bitmap into a vector by tracing the image, attempting to simulate the look of the bitmap.

TRACKING
Process of uniformly increasing or decreasing the space between all letters in a block of text. (See Kerning.)

TRANSFORM
Functions such as moving, scaling, or rotating an object.

TRANSPARENCY
The relative opacity of an object from 0% (invisible) to 100% (fully opaque).

TWEENING
Process of adding intermediate frames of animation, between two keyframes, in a program such as Adobe Flash, to create subtle movement.

TYPEFACE
The set of characters created by a type designer, including uppercase and lowercase alphabetical characters, numbers, punctuation, and special characters. A single typeface contains many fonts, at different sizes and styles.

TYPE FAMILY
A group of typefaces of the same basic design, but with different weights and proportions. Helvetica Regular, Helvetica Oblique, Helvetica Bold, and Helvetica Bold Oblique could be a basic type family.

TYPOGRAPHY
Art and technique of setting and arranging type with specifications provided by a designer or art director.

VECTOR EDITOR
Computer program such as Adobe Illustrator, FreeHand, or CorelDRAW used primarily to create and manipulate vector graphics.

VECTOR GRAPHICS
Vector files are resolution-independent graphic files composed of line and curve segments, created in such programs as Illustrator, FreeHand, and CorelDRAW. Vectors are described by a series of coordinates indicating the position of points and other attributes through simple mathematical descriptions. In a bitmap editor, each pixel is defined by numbers describing each pixel. A black-and-white ellipse in a vector drawing consists of numbers describing four anchor points, a number describing the radius, the color, and the characteristics of the path. This makes files that are usually smaller. The same circle in a bitmap editor is described by a number of up to 32 numerals describing each individual pixel.

VECTORIZATION
Conversion of a bitmap image to a vector generally through some form of tracing in a vector application.

Index

175

Acknowledgments

J.H. would like to thank Jen for waiting to travel to Pluto and
S.W. for the ultimate in patience.

S.W. thanks the contributing artists and designers, especially
Patrick Coyle, Charley Parker, Nigel Holmes, and Melinda
Rainsberger; Jack, for aiming so high; and Lesley and
Marin, for patience and love.

Picture Credits

Cover and flaps: © Ellen McAuslan, © Zeptonn (Jan Willem
Wennekes), © Alexandru Sacui, © Petra Stefankova, © Jannie
Ho, © Birgit Amadori, © Jon Burgerman, © Chisato Shinya,
© Dave Curd, © XDude, © Rian Hughes, © Colin Hayes,
© Patrick Coyle

Page 4 © Jonathan Rosenberg; Pages 6 and 7 © Onno Knuvers;
Pages 10 and 11 © Iker Ayestarán, © Rian Hughes, © Demian
Vogler; Pages 12 through 15 © Isabelle Dervaux, © Daniel
Pelavin; Pages 16 and 17 © Steven Withrow, © Dave Curd;
Pages 18 and 19 © and ™ Christopher Mills, © and ™ Helena
Jones, © Nate Piekos; Pages 20 and 21 © Von Glitschka;
Pages 42 and 43 © Birgit Amadori; Pages 44 and 45 © Jon
Burgerman; Pages 46 and 47 © Iker Ayestarán (see image
captions for client list); Pages 58 and 59 "Santa" © 2003 Jack
Harris, iPod® illustration, iStockphoto.com; Pages 66 and 67
© Brad Hamann (see image captions for client list); Pages 68
and 69 © Mar Hernández; Pages 70 and 71 © Chisato Shinya;
Pages 74 and 75 "April Fools" © 2003 Jack Harris; Pages 76
and 77 "Nor'easter" © 2004 Jack Harris; Pages 82 and 83
photography, AbleStock.com; Pages 84 and 85 "apple"
photograph, AbleStock.com; Pages 90 and 91 © Catalina
Estrada; Pages 92 and 93 © Nancy Stahl (see image captions
for client list); Pages 94 and 95 © Cristiano Siqueira; Pages 98
and 99 excerpt from I, Robot © 2005 Cory Doctorow; Page
100 and 101 excerpt from I, Robot © 2005 Cory Doctorow;
Pages 102 and 103 original illustration, Andrzej Windak,
iStockphoto.com; Pages 104 and 105 excerpt from I, Robot
© 2005 Cory Doctorow; Pages 100 and 111 © Rian Hughes
(see image captions for client list); Pages 112 and 113 © Mike
Quon and Designation, Inc.; Pages 114 and 115 © Zeptonn
(Jan Willem Wennekes) (see image captions for client list);
Pages 118 and 119 "video camera" illustration, iStockphoto.
com; Pages 120 and 121 "crystal" ball illustration, iStockphoto.
com; Pages 122 and 123 photograph of man, AbleStock.com,
"finger pointing" photograph, AbleStock.com, "bee"
illustration, © 2002 Jack Harris; Pages 124 and 125 "OSX or
XP" illustration © 2005 Art Lubalin; Pages 126 and 127 "frog"
photograph and "street sign" illustration, iStockphoto.com;
Pages 132 and 133 © Petra Stefankova; Pages 134 and 135 ©
Charlene Chua; Pages 136 and 137 © Ellen McAuslan; Pages
140 and 141 © Patrick Coyle and Komikwerks; Pages 142 and
143 © Patrick Coyle and Komikwerks, © Darren Coyle and
Scott Boyce, The World of Quest © Jason Kruse; Pages 144 and
145 © CEDIM (reprinted with permission), © Federico Jordán
Gomez; Pages 146 and 147 © Colin Hayes; Pages 148 and 149
© Nigel Holmes; Pages 150 and 151 © Dale Glasgow; Pages
152 through 155 © Clio Chiang, © Kathi Käppel, © XDude;
Pages 156 and 157 © Alexandru Sacui, © Brownstone Monkey
Productions Inc.; Pages 158 and 159 Sheesh ™ Jim Keplinger
and Steve Musgrave, © Jannie Ho (see image captions for
client list); Page 160 and 161 © Russell Tate; Pages 162
and 163 © Melinda Rainsberger